How to Have a Champagne Wedding on a Buck's Fizz Budget

Sarah Traynor

GILL & MACMILLAN

Gill & Macmillan Ltd
Hume Avenue, Park West, Dublin 12
with associated companies throughout the world
www.gillmacmillan.ie
© Sarah Traynor 2007
978 07171 4113 5
Index compiled by Cover to Cover
Design by Anú Design
Print origination by Carole Lynch
Printed by ColourBooks Ltd, Dublin

*The paper used in this book comes from the wood pulp
of managed forests. For every tree felled, at least one tree
is planted, thereby renewing natural resources.*

A CIP catalogue record for this book
is available from the British Library.

5 4 3 2 1

For John, and my little writing companion Tommy

The Bargain

My true love hath my heart, and I have his,
By just exchange one for another given.
I hold his dear, and mine he cannot miss,
There never was a better bargain driven.

Sir Philip Sidney (1554–1586)

Contents

Acknowledgments   ix

Introduction   xi

Decision Time – What, Where and When?

1.	The Anatomy of a Wedding	1
	Interview: Eddie Hobbs on Financing Your Wedding	5
2.	Shopping: General Tips	10
	Interview: Alex French, Author of *DOT.ie: A Practical Guide to Using the Internet in Ireland*	15
3.	The Ceremony	19
4.	The Reception Venue	29
	Interview: Georgina Campbell on Romantic Weddings and Honeymoons	38

Throwing a Party

5.	Food	43
6.	Champagne, Buck's Fizz and Wine	51
	Interview: Paolo Tullio on Choosing Your Wine	56
7.	The Cake	59
8.	Entertainment	65
	Interview: Ruairi Finnegan on Hiring a DJ	69

Looking Good

9.	The Dress	73
10.	The Bridal Party — Seven Savings	81
11.	Accessories — Nine Ways to Save Money	84

12.	Ten Things about Rings	87
13.	Shoes	91
	Interview: Make-up — Annie Gribbon, Founder of Face2 Make-up	94
	Interview: Hairdressing — Anthony Murray — Irish Icon Hall of Fame Award 2006	97

Wedding Styles

14.	Flowers and Decorations	103
	Interview: Ruth and Ultan from Appassionata Flowers	115
15.	Favours	120
16.	Themes and Inspirations	124
17.	Stationery	129
18.	The Car	135

Recording the Day

19.	Photography	141
20.	Video/DVD	145
	Interview: Janet and Ben from Glass Eye Productions	149

Further Afield

21.	Getting Married Abroad	155
22.	The Honeymoon	164
23.	How to Have a Champagne Hen on a Buck's Fizz Budget Advice from Jenni Woolfson of Posh Fizz	170

Resources

| 24. | Research Tools and Web Summary | 177 |

| Index | | 187 |

Acknowledgments

I would like to thank everyone at Gill & Macmillan, in particular Fergal, D, Nicki and Sinead; Graham for the perfect cover design; Karen for the interior design; and Aideen for all the great suggestions. A big thank you to those who contributed their wisdom to the book: Eddie Hobbs, Alex French, Georgina Campbell, Paolo Tullio, Ruairi Finnegan, Annie Gribbon, Anthony Murray, Andrea Caldecourt, Ruth and Ultan, Janet and Ben and Jenni Woolfson. I would also like to thank the newlyweds for sharing their valuable tips and a sincere thank you to two magicmums, Fiona and Claire, for the help and ideas. My own wedding would not have been so happy and fun without the love and support from my family and all my enthusiastic guests!

But above all I need to thank my wonderful husband John for his constant encouragement and patience during the writing of this book — and for the regular supply of chocolate and coffee!

Introduction

Congratulations! So you are getting married. This is a very simple process: you give the State three months notice of your intention to marry and, depending on your choice of ceremony — civil or religious — you follow the legal procedures required in advance. You pick a date and on that day you meet before witnesses to marry. Every other layer, frill or flower is added by choice, *your* choice.

Yet, as we all know, from such simple seeds monsters can grow. Traditional Irish weddings have earned a reputation as high-stress, overpriced and over-rated events. Never before has the idea of getting married become so unromantic, as couples bang figures into calculators, sometimes tossing between buying a home *or* getting married. Wedding message boards are littered with tales of financial strain, family pressure, ridiculous excess and inevitable tears.

But it doesn't have to be this way. So, for those of you who want a big traditional wedding without the fear of bankruptcy, for those of you looking for good value at a fair price, for those of you eager to stretch that hard-earned budget and who refuse to part with thousands of euro in exchange for shoddy service and soggy vegetables — this book is for you.

Who am I? And what makes me such an expert?

I don't work in the wedding industry. I don't have a marketing degree or run a business. My only qualification in this area is as a consumer and as an aspiring journalist with a nose for investigation. I had a traditional Irish wedding with 170 guests. I saved in many areas in order to have the numbers and the venue I wanted. The day was everything I hoped for, even the weather co-operated. In the lead-up I did well to stay focused and good-humoured and I managed to avoid becoming completely overwhelmed with what I was doing. Moving from one shock price to the next, I nervously punched figures into a worn-out calculator. I was rarely happy with what I saw. The prices being charged for wedding services in this country are astronomical. My search for quality at a 'fair' price was long. Apparently, the market charges what people are prepared to pay. And where has that left the newly engaged? Let down by a legacy of overspending. Paying photographers about a month's salary for a day of their time. Forking out the price of a second-hand car for a band to play easy listening for two hours. What quantum leap occurs in the short stroll from Top Shop to the nearest bridal shop? Women who normally baulk at a €300 price tag on evening wear are suddenly paying €1,500 for a dress!

I passed through the maze that is planning a wedding in Ireland and went on honeymoon a little dazed and confused. On return I surveyed the damage. And of course, despite some excellent money-saving ideas, there was still a major hole in our bank accounts. We knew we would be still paying for our wedding long after our tans had faded. 'Where did we concede too easily?' 'Where did we simply waste money?' 'Where could we have done better?' My doodling turned into paragraphs, curious phone calls, hundreds of web searches and before I knew it I was talking to a publisher. What you are reading now is *the* book to help you navigate the maze you are about to enter.

This book will show you how to find products and services that you need for your wedding at reasonable prices. As we all know, the devil is in the details. I will suggest alternatives in every area of planning, and encourage you to question preconceived ideas and consider other options. This book will stir your imagination and get you to unleash that creative side you know you have. And, most importantly, this book will encourage you to **get online!**

> **Where did I save?**
> - Made a saving of €1000 buying my dress online.
> - Bought two designer bridesmaids' dresses from another bride, saving €700.
> - Used a cake from Marks and Spencer.
> - Stormed the sales for shoes and accessories.
> - Bought antique rings.
> - Asked friends for the gift of music at our ceremony.
> - Made hair decorations.
>
> These, along with some other savings, allowed us to afford to have all the guests we wanted in the venue of our choice.

What's so different about this book?

Bookshelves are packed full with books on etiquette, speeches, wedding music and legal and religious guides. Where is the book that deals with the subject everyone wants to hear about: 'How can I have a successful wedding on the budget I have to work with?'

The sole focus of this book is to show you how to have a champagne wedding on a buck's fizz budget. This is not a guide to getting married; it will not list legal procedures or hold pages of readings and sample speeches. It will, however, point you to the abundant sources where you can find this information on the internet or in the library.

During the planning and organising of my wedding I discovered many interesting websites. In the time since, during the research for this book, I explored further, finding more and more little gems. As I clicked from site to site I followed links like crumbs leading me to the wonderful gingerbread house that is value for money! Some of the sites are great — I know, from using them regularly — others impressed me and appear to offer value for money. Although I have checked through these sites and I have contacted many of the people that run the sites, I can't take responsibility for any of your use of these sites or the services they provide. All websites are copyright and the property of their original owners. None of these sites was mentioned in exchange for presents, promotions, free chocolate or cake. Although I do like cake.

Finally, this book is for anyone getting married. Why? Because whether you have €3,000 or €30,000 to spend, as a customer you have a *right* to expect value for money and, of course, because everyone loves a bargain!

Decision Time — What, Where and When?

Chapter One

The Anatomy of a Wedding

Graphically a wedding, like many things, looks straightforward enough. The bubbles from left to right represent all the elements that make up a typical wedding: bridal party looking good; sending invitations; ceremony with guests, music and some decoration; recording the day; a party with food, wine and maybe some entertainment; often followed by a trip. Get all these elements right and you are guaranteed a wonderful day. Right?

Probably. This may be a simplistic way of looking at an event but it is an important start. Breaking your day down into digestible chunks can make all of the planning less daunting. Assigning a deadline to each area and delegating between yourselves who does what will simplify organising a wedding considerably. It certainly beats making endless complicated lists, phone numbers on Post-its crumpled at the bottom of a handbag or screaming at each other a month before the wedding when it all gets too much.

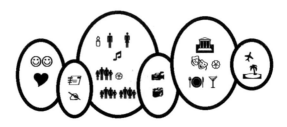

If each area is given just a little research time early on, then you will be able to spare yourself the last-minute flurry of paying high prices for mediocre services just to tick an item off a list. It *is* possible to maintain affordability without compromising on quality or style, but it is essential to allow yourself that time for sourcing and preparation. It's never too early to start your preparations.

In this first chapter, 'Anatomy of a Wedding', I will take a *bride's eye view* of the day and the wedding industry you are now part of. This should help by giving you a general feel for the task ahead of you. The first thing to remember is that hotels, suppliers and shops all *need* your business, never forget that. There is rarely any repeat custom when it comes to weddings and this can result in poor service, but with the advent of the internet and wonderful message boards, you can now find and work from recommendations from other couples.

More about this later. First, let's look at the starting point, the real ball and chain, the one thing you can't change much …

The Budget

Like any big decisions, making choices about what you can and can't have at your wedding will be difficult. You want your wedding day to be right. Not just *right* — perfect! You want to indulge yourselves a little too, and why not? The marketing machine at work on you from the moment you open a bridal magazine is massive and hungry for customers, playing to any insecurities you may have, trying to lure you into a fairytale. Added to this, you may worry that there are certain expectations held by family or friends of what a wedding day should be like. Yet at the same time you have to be realistic and make sensible decisions based on the budget you have to work with.

In Ireland today, balancing your dream day and your real budget is not an easy task. With increasing numbers getting married every year there is a high demand for wedding services, and prices have risen significantly, often well out of the reach of many couples. So, as your planning starts and the price lists start coming through the door, you might find yourself getting a little stressed out.

But don't worry, with a little imagination, some good research and a bit of neck, you might surprise yourself with what you can actually achieve with *your* budget.

> I got married in May this year for under €4,000!... and it was the best day of our lives. Our 28 guests are still talking about it. We had a very strict budget to stick to as we just bought a house and have two small children. Things were so tight I only got my dress two weeks beforehand! We did everything ourselves, the only things we didn't do were cook the meal, bake the cake, play the music or take the photos. It was an amazing day. I washed my hair at home, ran up to the hairdressers to get it tied back nicely. Did make-up myself at home with all my usual stuff! I got some nice nails in Boots and stuck them on that morning. I don't understand why all these silly women go on the way they do getting married, fake nails, tans etc and half the time I think they look ridiculous, some of those rip-off dresses are hideous! People are crazy having big expensive weddings . . .
>
> **Sharon, Dublin**

Wish List and Budget List

Get out a page and write 'Wish List' at the top. Ditch the calculator for this. This is where you use the right side of your brain, the imaginative side where your creative thoughts and dreams come from. Write down your priorities for the day — how you picture it: a traditional hotel 'do' or a trip to Vegas on your own? An intimate meal in a country house or a helicopter ride to a castle . . . ? Write it all down! Your dreams are important and they are the best starting point. You might be surprised at how close you can get.

Now, get out another page and welcome your logical and analytical left brain into the conversation. We're talking money here. Write down your monthly earnings and monthly outgoings, then find the bottom line — the spare money at the end of the month (if there is any!). Scribble next to it any savings either of you might have or can generate in the coming months (you will find some savings ideas in this chapter). Tot the figures up and there you have it — your budget. You may decide to talk to your bank manager about a little extra. Eddie Hobbs looks at that option in the interview opposite.

> If you own your home, why not rent a room? A little sacrifice of space in the year before your wedding could seriously aid your cause (see *daft.ie*). Check out *revenue.ie* for details of the tax-free rent-a-room scheme.

> Put yourself forward for as much overtime as you can get in work. If you have spare time why not consider taking on some casual work? This could help your wedding fund significantly. People are doing it to save deposits for a house, why not do it for a year to save for your wedding? The website *nixers.com* has everything from doing Santa at Christmas to Saturday work in a call centre.

Remember, the two lists will most definitely evolve over time, especially as you read this book and realise the savings that can be made. By weighing up what is most important, you can allocate spending most efficiently, saving in areas of less importance while spending more in others. And you never know, you might be lucky with a bonus in work or an unexpected cheque from time to time, which will help that bottom line. Put your discoveries into a notebook and keep the notebook somewhere you both have access to, jot down savings, write in prices . . . if everything budget-related is in the one place it makes life easier. Now, to really get what is on your wish list, or at least as close as possible with the budget you have to work with, you will need to research well. Eddie Hobbs will get you started here with some solid financial advice . . .

Eddie Hobbs on Financing Your Wedding

Financial guru and whistleblower on the rip-off culture in Ireland talks weddings.

Many couples book their wedding one to two years in advance. Do you have any basic savings ideas for couples in the lead-up to the day?

Eddie: Over short terms like these you can't really afford to take investment risks like buying gold or shares in the expectation of a bull market in the interim, so cash deposits are needed. But there are vast differences in rates for the small saver. Best to go for an account that tracks up with any rise in interest rates, ideally linked to the ECB rate, which is expected to rise throughout 2007. The best deals for ad hoc deposits are on-line accounts from Northern Rock and Rabo Direct and, for regular monthly savings, Bank of Scotland and AIB, but check the terms and conditions. Over time these tips can change but if you visit *askaboutmoney.com* and look for the Best Buys section you'll get the up-to-date info you need.

Given that fixed costs (such as band, DJ, cake, clothing) are similar for large and small weddings, and that most guests more than cover the cost of their meal with gifts, is it a good idea to make your wedding party as large as possible? Is a small wedding a false economy?

Eddie: If the 'Cash Gifts Only' slogan has gained traction among reasonably well-off relatives and pals, you might break even on the deal the more you add. Couples who do the math might find, for example, that each extra invite adds say €60 to the variable costs (food and booze) but, with an average cash gift of say €100, adds €40 to recovering fixed costs. The higher the average cash gift you can get and the greater the number of guests, the closer you'll get to break-even or, heaven forbid, a profit! But this approach should not be tried among those with notoriously tight relatives — you know the types that want the knees-up for the cheapest fondue set.

What advice do you have for couples considering taking out a loan to cover the costs of the day?

Eddie: It's easier said than done to try to avoid borrowing, typically at rates between 7% and 12% on term loans, or worse, on credit cards for last-minute costs where rates are up to 18%. The problem is that hard finance sits uneasily with romance and couples often don't really properly consider the huge set-back that thirty thousand could be until it's too late to call a halt, as fretting mammies add more and more to the list. Ideally the parents and friends should be encouraged to give Cash Gifts Only.

With high prices, some would say rip-off prices, for many wedding-related goods and services, do you have any bargaining tips for couples trying to get a good deal with suppliers?

Eddie: This really comes down to human nature. Lots of businesses supplying this market know that their customers are vulnerable and in a romantic daze — often the type that might think that haggling is offensive to the whole exercise. Get past that feeling and haggle. Don't ever take the first price you are offered unless it's genuinely unbeatable. Always leverage the competitive forces in the market, tell the supplier that you are shopping around but be careful too because nothing in the world cannot be made a little cheaper and just a little worse. Think laterally . . . could you get a few cheap flights to, say, Budapest and get a cracker of a wedding dress for half the cost of one here? With the photographer, insist on owning the copyright on your snaps. Some photographers might baulk, but if they do, just tell them you'll go elsewhere. Never bluff — an experienced haggler will see it in your eyes or hear it in your voice, so mean it.

When we got engaged, I started ringing around for prices. I estimated what we wanted at about €10,000. We had everything pretty much picked out but then we bought our house. On top of that we found it hard to get the money together for all the bits and pieces, even with both sets of parents paying for the reception! Then we had a baby ... So the thought of handing out huge amounts of money for just one day killed us. So we completely scaled everything down and in the end, in total, our wedding cost just over €1000! And that was with €600 of it going on the reception. I bought my wedding dress and bridesmaid dress on sale in Hickeys in Henry Street. I actually had my son christened after we said our vows, so it was great value for money! You don't need to spend huge amounts of money for it to be a good and memorable day, as we all found out.

Sheila, Dublin

Decision Time — First Considerations

With your wish list and budget lists in hand, you will need to start considering the initial decisions: What type of wedding? Where to have it? Who to invite? How to achieve all this within your budget? The following general points are worth discussing together before getting into the details.

The whole day matters

People often put so much effort into the evening celebrations, where they try to make a big 'impact', that they forget that perhaps the most important impact made on the day is the ceremony itself. You, like many couples, will probably find it to be the calmest and most enjoyable part of the day. It is also the least expensive. So here the best spend is on time. Chat to your celebrant, choose words, poetry and readings that speak to you, spend time picking out music and thinking of ways to brighten up the church or hall.

Size

From the guest list to the bridal party, the budget for any type of wedding is largely reflective of how big you go. Generally, the bigger the wedding, the higher the cost — but this doesn't make guests impossible to fit within a clever budget. A decision to leave children out or co-workers can be politely defended by a numbers cap enforced by the venue. Ironically, given the fixed costs of every wedding (food, band, dress, etc.), inviting *more* guests along with some subtle encouragements for cash gifts can actually help reduce net costs and work out more economical overall. Generally, however, the reduction of a guest list, even the size of your bridal party, can impact greatly on your budget and, therefore, on the rest of your choices. Of course, if you want a very small wedding you are already off to a good start.

Time of year

The time of year you choose to get married will affect the style and economics of the wedding in many ways, including location of the reception, honeymoon destinations, wedding theme and prices. According to the Central Statistics Office, the most popular month for weddings is August, the least popular being January and February. You have more bargaining power during off-peak times, as the services are least in demand and discounts are often easy to come by. Saturday is also confirmed as the most popular day. So, not surprisingly, with over 25,000 weddings in the Republic of Ireland and Northern Ireland per year, you often need to book a hotel over one year in advance to secure a Saturday. So consider alternative days. It is hard to understand why bank holiday Mondays are not a more popular choice for couples. This is a day off for most, unlike the second most popular day, Friday. Many churches will not perform weddings on a Sunday but if you are having a blessing or party on return from a wedding abroad this would be a good day to choose. It is a day off for many and services are easier and cheaper to book as they are less in demand.

Location

In making the decision on where to hold your wedding, good research is essential. Putting time aside to find the right venue for your needs will prove invaluable. Look for recommendations, visit venues prepared for a wedding, taste the food, get clear detailed price lists and ask as many questions as you can think of. You can eliminate a lot of the stress of organising this event by booking a good professional service you can rely on.

Keep an open mind. Check out alternative ideas while you are at it. If you are prepared to go further afield you may save money, for example meeting halfway between where you are both from could mean meeting in a more rural, less expensive location.

Believe it or not, one of the best ways to save money is probably to marry abroad. The reception and honeymoon are rolled into one and you are unlikely to have to invite as many guests. If you would miss the bit of fuss at home, an increasingly popular option is marrying abroad and booking a buffet with some entertainment back home for an evening celebration.

In the next few chapters you will find many secrets to achieving the wedding of your dreams. The most important thing to do first though is to accept the budget you have to work with, no matter how small, and enjoy discovering how far you can stretch it. The preparations for your wedding day can be almost as much fun as the day itself!

> I was in the hospital A&E dept on the morning of my wedding, so the most important thing for me was to get to the cathedral to be married, the rest was a bonus. I was an hour late, but I made it!
>
> **Rachel, Galway**

 # Webguide

daft.ie
nixers.com
revenue.ie

Chapter Two

Shopping: General Tips

All shopping trips should be preceded by a visit to one of the excellent online wedding forums for a chat. A quick search on *weddingsonline.ie/ discussion*, for example, will provide you with information on all the latest bargains and special offers. For further details on the research you can do, see the resource section at the end of the book.

A trip down the high street: four of the best shops for bridalwear

National and international retail chains are increasingly offering more wedding services in an effort to enjoy a piece of the pie that is the bridal market. This is a massive help to anyone looking for an affordable wedding. Like everything, department stores can match the look of the catwalks at a fraction of the price. Here I will look at the leaders in this area: Debenhams, Monsoon, Next and Marks & Spencer, all of which have stores in Ireland. If you can't find something in the Irish shops, you should check out their UK websites, as they often deliver to Ireland.

For purchases in Sterling check out *xe.com* to see if you are getting a good deal. Remember too that postage will add to the price.
For your nearest branches check out *goldenpages.ie*.

DEBENHAMS
debenhamsweddings.com

Debenhams are definitely the leaders in dressing the bridal party, with their wedding dress collection (prices approx €230–€800) and their excellent selection of bridesmaids' dresses in both classic and alternative styles. Bridal menswear and children's wear are also available at reasonable prices.

They offer personalised wedding stationery which is on display in the store. Their website is excellent and it will guide you through all the items on offer, or if you call into the store you can pick up a wedding product brochure.

MARKS & SPENCER
marksandspencer.com

Wedding dresses The high street chain very recently launched their first wedding dress range at selected stores. Priced at €130–€190, they are part of a wider collection that includes bridesmaids' dresses and formal suits for grooms. Bridal dresses are made from fabrics such as chiffon, overlaid lace and crepes in white and vintage cream. They have also launched their first collection of Truly You bridal lingerie. The range includes a selection of basques, knickers, bras and suspenders.

Cakes This is the place to get your cake. These immaculate cakes are fantastic when dressed with flowers or feathers or even chocolate! You have a choice of fruit or butter sponge. If the butter sponge is not available in the Irish store you visit, ask for it to be ordered in. They regularly have 'three layers for the price of two' offers and you will pay as little as €75 for your cake. The manager of the hotel I had my wedding in commented that her favourite cakes were those from Marks & Spencer because 'they look so perfect'. The hotel florist decorated it free of charge and it looked beautiful. Place your bouquets next to the cake before the meal for some extra colour.

Invitations Marks & Spencer recently launched their new invitation range with a CD-ROM for you to personalise them yourself. You will also find simple white guest books to pass around during your meal.

Hair and jewellery Marks & Spencer are known for their excellent jewellery. If you are looking for pearl styles or evening costume jewellery, this really should be the first place you look. Many of the items are aimed specifically at the bridal market, including feather pieces and white and ivory handbags.

Books You will also find some reasonably priced books on wedding themes such as decorating for your day, poems, readings and speech preparation.

Shoes You can rely on Marks & Spencer to have a selection of simple shoes perfect for you or your bridesmaids. And if you wait for the sale, like I did, you make even more of a saving.

NEXT
nextdirectory.ie

Next stock bridesmaids' dresses that look as good as many of the much more expensive designer dresses on the market. The bridal selection is better in the UK — something to keep in mind if you are making a trip up North — but you can be sure the range in Ireland will only get better and better.

Bridal party Bridesmaids' dresses are around €90. The wedding shoes are all around €36 and you will find styles suitable for bride and bridesmaids. You will also find beautiful bridal jewellery, hair pieces and feather capes. For more contemporary evening style bridesmaids' dresses, they have a wide selection of suitable evening wear. Have a look at their black satin corset dress at around €80. Check out the prom dresses too, which can be perfect for bridesmaids. They stock men's wedding wear too.

Little ones Next sell ivory flower girl dresses (€52–€55) and matching pretty shoes, or beautiful baby-pink flower girl dresses for €30. They even sell baby christening dresses (€36) which would look wonderful at a wedding.

Practicalities As well as clothing, Next also sell leather wedding albums (€36), fitting approximately 100 7x5 photographs, and wedding guest books (€19).

MONSOON
monsoon.co.uk

Monsoon is the queen of the high street when it comes to wedding dresses. They do a wonderful range of jewellery and flower girl and page boy outfits, but their real speciality is in wedding dresses that blow many of the designer alternatives out of the water. If you see something you like online, check with your nearest Monsoon store before ordering to see if it is available in the shop, or they may be able to order it in. For accessories and children's clothing you don't even have to leave your house — the UK website delivers to the Republic of Ireland for €11.

Wedding dresses There is a good selection from €200 to €300. Alongside the traditional styles they do some quite unusual gowns that will appeal to a bride looking for something a little bit different, with crochet, silk taffeta and embroidery. Some of the dresses are suitable for a less formal wedding or for anyone getting married abroad.

Bridesmaids' dresses These dresses are top quality but they are not the cheapest. The prices range from €200 to €300. Again you can't beat Monsoon for *something different*—alongside the traditional styles some of these dresses have beautiful embroidery, bows and belts, with many in vibrant colours, perfect for the more fun style wedding. Be sure to have a look in the non-bridal sections here too because often evening wear dresses are suitable.

Little ones The flower girl dresses are not cheap, but they are cheaper than designer dresses. You will pay €90 and upwards. Party dresses, which are pretty much the same idea, are cheaper at around €60. Party shoes are around €30, again pricey. If the child's parents want to invest in a pair for the season, point them here. For winter weddings Monsoon do nice white or ivory tights for around €7.

Bonus Monsoon also stock cute white **feather pens** for about €10 which would look great for photographs, signing the register or passing around with your guest book.

> If you really must use a credit card when shopping, why not become a credit card tart? By hopping from one card to another it is possible to go twelve months plus without paying any interest on purchases. Some providers offer 0% on purchase and balance transfers for six to nine months, for example, Ulster Bank Zinc nine months and AIB six months. You could use cash gifts to clear the balance. Beware: Standard credit card APRs of up to 18% kick in when the introductory offer expires.

And the rest . . .

For bridal party hair, jewellery, feather shrugs and beading, try **Claire's Accessories** and **Accessorize**. **Arnott's** also have a wide selection of children's party clothing and their costume jewellery is worth a look too. Jewellery in **Brown Thomas** ladies wear department is surprisingly well priced. **Eason's** is great for stationery and candles.

Of course some of the best shops are those without shop fronts — the online variety. In the next section Alex French gives some practical tips about how useful the internet will be in your search for value.

✳ ✳ ✳

Alex French on Using the Internet

Author of *DOT.ie: A Practical Guide to Using the Internet in Ireland*

Shopping online is a bit like shopping in a big foreign city — of course it's possible to get ripped off, but if you do a little research and use common sense, you can get great bargains with little risk.

One of the most important things when you shop online is to do your homework about the website. Ask other people (in person or on online forums or bulletin boards) what sites they've used and what their experiences were. Did they have any problems? Were their questions answered promptly? This is good advice for *any* online shopping, but it's particularly important when you're shopping for high-value things like a wedding dress.

Most online shopping problems relate to shipping, returns or payment, so pay particular attention to the site's customer service policies before you order.

Sending your credit card details off into the depths of the internet can be daunting, but rest assured that if you take a few simple precautions you shouldn't have any problems.

People are sometimes concerned about hackers intercepting their credit card details as they're transmitted to the website; you can guard against this by making sure that the website uses a 'secure' payment page. This means that all the information you send to a site is securely encrypted while it travels over the internet. You can make sure a page is secure by looking for a small padlock icon on the bottom of the page. You can also click on the padlock to see more details.

In reality, the risk of your credit card details being intercepted while they're being sent over the network is pretty small. When credit card numbers are stolen online, they're usually taken from the online records

15

of well-meaning sites that don't take proper security precautions. It's the equivalent of someone breaking into a shop and stealing your details from their filing cabinet. There's not much you can do to guard against this except to make sure the site you're buying from is reputable and has a good reputation among past shoppers. Some large online shops (like *Amazon.com*) also guarantee that they'll give you a refund if your card details are stolen from them.

You should also remember that your best defence against credit card fraud (on- or off-line) is to regularly check your credit card statements. If you see anything unusual, contact your card issuer immediately. If you're careful with your credit cards and notify your card company promptly of any problems, you will usually not have to pay for a fraudulent charge. (You may have to pay a small amount, usually less than €100, of a disputed transaction. The details depend on your card issuer.)

The Irish Payment Services Organisation has a good website about preventing credit card and ATM card fraud at *safecard.ie*.

Once you've found a site you want to buy from, take a few minutes before actually placing the order to check some basics: are there 'real' contact details (like a phone number and address) on the website? What's the refund policy? And are they a member of any online verification schemes, such as the BBBOnline for US shops, which aims to promote safe online shopping (details are available at *bbbonline.org*).

When I'm going to order something high-value or book a hotel online, I often make direct contact with the vendor first (by email or phone) to see how they respond. Even if I don't have any important questions, I'll ask them something simple just to see if they answer quickly and sound helpful. This can give you a feeling for the quality of their customer service — or if they don't respond you'll know to look elsewhere.

Buying on eBay is a little more complicated than buying from an online shop, but not much — and can get you some great bargains. To bid for something on eBay you need to sign up for an account, which involves providing your credit card details. This is to try and verify your identity, and you won't be charged anything at the registration stage.

When you're buying on eBay, remember that you're dealing with the individual selling the goods, and not eBay, so you need to make sure you trust them. eBay's site has a built-in trust system called Feedback, which lets you see how other people rated the seller and how many things they've sold. This is shown on each auction page and you can click on it to see details of the seller's past auctions. A good seller will have close to 100% positive feedback and not too many negative comments.

Be sure to read the description of the goods carefully — many things on eBay are second-hand and may not be in perfect condition. You should also check whether the seller will ship to Ireland, and what the shipping costs will be (these are usually in addition to the final auction price). If you're in any doubt, use the 'Ask the seller a question' feature to make sure *before* you bid since *a bid is a binding contract!*

Because most things on eBay are being auctioned, not sold for a fixed price, you need to decide the absolute maximum you'd be willing to spend and place one bid for that amount. The website will only offer the seller as much as necessary to outbid other people, up to the maximum amount you specified.

Once you win an auction, you have to pay the seller. Most people on eBay use the PayPal system to pay. This is a service that transfers money between people without revealing your credit card details to the recipient. Although this means the seller doesn't see your card number, you aren't always protected if something goes wrong. Despite this, PayPal is the safest way to pay if you use eBay. You should *never* use Western Union or a bank draft to pay — if anything goes wrong it's practically impossible to get your money back if you've paid in these ways.

If you're planning a wedding abroad you'll often have little choice but to use the internet for booking at least some parts of your trip. If you're searching for the perfect venue, food or other wedding necessities in a foreign city, the net is by far the easiest way to do your research. And as you've probably found out by now, the best deals are often found online.

However, there's a big difference between finding a supplier and agreeing the details with them. If you have specific requirements, you'd be well advised to communicate directly with the supplier (either by email or preferably by phone) to make sure they understand exactly what you want. This is particularly true if there's a language barrier — if there's any possibility of a misunderstanding, you want to work it out well in advance! This is true for travel arrangements, too — it's fine to book flights directly on an airline's website, but if you want to be sure that your hotel room has a sea view, contact them directly, no matter what their website says!

If something goes wrong

If you have any problems with an online purchase, here's what to do:

- Contact the seller directly to try and resolve the dispute.
- Keep a record of all your communication with the seller, including emails.
- If you've bought from an online seller within the EU, the European Consumer Centre can help you resolve the issue. See *eccdublin.ie*.
- If you have a problem with an eBay purchase, use their Safety Centre to report the problem.
- If you can't resolve the issue with the seller, contact your card issuer (usually your bank) to dispute the transaction. Have all the transaction details to hand.

Shopping Online?
Visit *myus.com*.
Your own US mailing address . . . from anywhere in the world! With this packaging and mailing service you can shop from US companies that don't ship overseas.

Webguide

amazon.com	*nextdirectory.ie*
bbbonline.org	*safecard.ie*
debenhamsweddings.com	*simplyweddings.com*
ebay.ie	*tab.ie*
eccdublin.ie	*theknot.com*
goldenpages.ie	*weddingsonline.ie*
hitched.co.uk	*xe.com*
ivoryandlace.com	
marksandspencer.com	
monsoon.co.uk	
myus.com	

Chapter Three

The Ceremony

In advance of your wedding day, be it by religious or civil service, you will need to deal with the legal and religious requirements. Once you have met with your celebrant or registrar before the day and the legal and religious paperwork is completed, then the best spend you can make here is on *time*. Time spent preparing your ceremony, adding a personal touch to the service, picking out some of your favourite music and brightening up the ceremony space. There are some excellent resources dealing with the legal and religious aspects of preparing for marriage, which are listed at the back of the book. The main emphasis of this chapter is on planning your ceremony well to ensure it is a part of the day that you and your guests thoroughly enjoy.

☼ First Decisions

You should first visit *citizensinformation.ie*. Once you are sure that you have the capacity to marry and have fulfilled the notification requirements, you can decide how you wish to marry in Ireland. You may choose a registry office marriage or opt for marriage by religious ceremony.

Church

If you want a church service, visit *gettingmarried.ie* for information on the time frames, legal requirements and for general advice. This website is very easy to navigate. From a budgeting perspective having a church wedding should not be very expensive; most people like to put aside some money to decorate the church with some flowers, bows or candles. You should also make a contribution to your priest on the day. If it is not your parish church you may also be requested to pay a church fee which can be anything up to €600.

Registry

The cost of a civil marriage is approximately €100. After that, whether or not you decide to decorate the space is up to you and, of course, the registrar. To contact the **General Registrar's Office** phone (090) 6632900 or visit *groireland.ie*. Registry weddings are very quick — they can be over in as little as five minutes.

> If you are in Northern Ireland visit *groni.gov.uk* or phone The Marriage Section (028) 90252000.

A bit of both

You could have the best of both worlds and enjoy a civil wedding followed by a more personal ceremony afterwards, perhaps a 'blessing'. The advantage of taking this route is there are no restraints on what you can do. You could follow the legal aspect of the day with a blessing in your local forest, Maid Marion style, or simply repeat your vows at the top table at your hotel. As exchanging the rings is not a requirement at a civil service you could do this later in the day.

Already married

There is a long tradition of 'church blessings' in this country where Irish people who have married in civil ceremonies in the UK, the USA, Australia, etc. marry in a religious ceremony the next time they are home.

> In more recent times couples are following the legal formality with humanist wedding ceremonies. Humanism is the belief that we can live good lives without religious or superstitious beliefs. For more details about humanism, or having a humanist ceremony, visit *irish-humanists.org*.

☺ Self-sufficient

No amount of money can liven up a dull ceremony. What I mean here is that the more thought you put into your choices — choice of content, reflections and the music — the more personal the day will feel for you and your guests.

Join in Ask your guests to participate in the ceremony. Put the words of the songs into a booklet and ask the celebrant to encourage guests to sing. Everyone feels part of the ceremony, it creates a great atmosphere and it is free! You could also ask your friends who play instruments or who can sing well to participate as a gift to you on the day.

Personal touch You will find books in your local library or bookshop with readings, poems and songs suitable for the occasion.

Bringing decorations to the venue If you want to brighten up your ceremony space with flowers and candles, remember you can splash out a little more if you decide to double up by bringing them to the reception too. If it is a church wedding it is usually expected that you leave one or two displays on the altar for parishioners to enjoy. For a registry wedding there is usually a CD player available. It is recommended you visit the room in advance. For more information turn to Chapter Fourteen on 'Flowers and Decorations'.

> At our ceremony we had several singers and a brass band. I was in the college folk group and they are still my close friends, and my husband still played occasionally with the brass band from his Boys' Brigade days. So our fabulous church music cost nothing! It was a brilliant day, and the involvement of friends and family in the actual wedding itself made it very special.
>
> **Vanya, Dublin**

Good Timing

Be punctual You have probably been a guest at a wedding where the bride has been late. Anything past fifteen minutes is starting to push it. It is a bad start to the day to have your guests and priest/registrar waiting thirty minutes and it will knock the schedule off for the entire day. If you are inviting elderly people or children to your wedding, for their sake you should avoid delaying the time between the ceremony and the dinner. Stay on target arriving at the church, with the length of your photo shoot and with the start time of the meal. This also ensures that if the speeches run over it won't impact too greatly on the evening's entertainment.

Keep it snappy! You don't have to turn your wedding into a Vegas style drive-through event but there is a happy medium. If you can't choose between a few songs it doesn't mean you should have them all! Anything over an hour for a wedding will have people looking at their watches no matter how enjoyable the experience. For church weddings, ask your priest and singer what the averages for content are and try and stick to them. However, don't make the mistake of running up and down the aisle. Walk slowly . . . no matter how nervous you feel, slow down, you don't want to be seated before the musicians have finished the first bar of music.

Seasonal blessings The time of year you have your wedding can have some valuable knock-on effects. At **Christmas,** there will probably be a nativity and a large sparkling tree, to which you could add some holly leaves, berries and candles along the window sills and aisles. That said, if you get married in March or May be aware that the church may be decorated with children's artwork as it will be Communion and Confirmation time.

Flowers in season As you will read in detail in Chapter Fourteen, it is best to choose flowers in season. Before doing so, take a long look at the room you are decorating. Larger, neutral, less expensive flowers might brighten up a large church much more than small rose displays. And if it is a small registry office, more delicate, detailed displays might suit the room better. Clever positioning of displays and the use of fillers mean you don't have to pay too much to brighten up your ceremony. In Chapter Fourteen Andrea from the UK Flowers Association and Ruth and Ultan of Appasionata Flowers advise on using flowers in season.

 ## Clever Tips

Sharing flowers For church weddings be sure to check with your priest to see if you are getting married on the same weekend as another couple. If so, get in touch; it could save you hundreds.

Ribbon Use bows on pew ends instead of flowers, it is much cheaper with a very similar effect. If you really want flowers, ask your florist to add a single gerbera or similar brightly coloured bloom to the bows the morning of the wedding. Lace or sheer ribbon draped from pew to pew will not only look great but it will help the usher when directing guests to their seats. Another advantage of this is that ribbon can be used to keep guests in from the aisle as sometimes guests step into the aisle to take photographs, obscuring the view of the professional photographer and videographer. (See *reasonableribbon.com*.)

Decorating with candles in the windows, across the altar, or on stands along the aisle will look beautiful, especially for winter weddings. Large church candles can be bought inexpensively online and in most department stores. You can prepare the base for the candle at home using some ivy from your garden and white flowers. Be sure to have someone gather them up afterwards so you can enjoy the candles for all those romantic winter evenings with your new spouse.

Using a florist Even if your budget is very small, a florist is invaluable on the day of your wedding. Some couples choose to decorate the church themselves, which is easier at Christmas (and sometimes necessary if the florists are closed). But on balance this may not be a valuable time spend on the morning of your wedding. The stress of doing this can easily outweigh the money savings. To save a little rather than paying the florist to do *everything*, why not take on a few of the easier tasks yourself such as making your own pew ends, which can be ready in advance to attach to the seats.

Red carpet Your church may already have one but most churches don't. Remember to budget about €100 for the rental and set-up of a red carpet. It is expensive but if your church is a little unkempt it does look good. Tiled churches or cathedrals often do not need a red carpet. To save here you could opt for a white fabric aisle runner, which you can buy on *myweddingbox.co.uk*.

> You can rent dramatic candelabras from many different suppliers such as *xena-productions.com*.

Baskets If you are having children in the bridal party it is a nice touch to give them each a basket of petals which they can toss as they go down the aisle. This might be a handy distraction for a nervous page boy! Your florist should be able to provide you with left-over petals.

Add some drama If you are having a church wedding, having a trumpet player announce your entrance and exit will create instant atmosphere as the congregation stands. It doesn't have to be an over-the-top marching band type trumpet; there are some beautiful trumpet solos. Check out the Trumpet Voluntary by Clarke (from the Prince of Denmark's March) in the music section on *webwedding.co.uk*. Mendelssohn's Wedding March is wonderful on the trumpet and is such exciting and fun music for you and your guests to exit to. It certainly got my heart thumping before I walked down the aisle. (Note: Sample music on these sites can sound a bit like something from a school concert but they are handy for giving you an idea of the tune.)

Keep it cheerful 'Ave Maria' is a beautiful song and used again and again (and again!) for weddings. But dare I say it; many people would agree with me that it is a bit depressing at such a happy event. To quote a wedding singer I spoke with recently, who will remain nameless: 'Please don't tell me I have to sing Ave Maria again . . . I am so bored of it.' Yes, weddings are solemn events but some cheerful music really is important too.

Practice makes perfect. Rehearsals are very handy as you should never assume people will know what to do. Practise with your bridesmaids how to hold the bouquets as you walk *slowly* down the aisle. In many of my pictures we are all holding the bouquets differently, which doesn't look great. The photographer may not point this out. Have rehearsals for readers; there is nothing worse than the sound of someone mumbling a reading into the microphone, so make sure your readers read it aloud at least once. And have a rehearsal for both of you; you will feel much more confident about things if you have had a dummy run.

◖D Something Different

Reform of the Irish marriage law is imminent following the Civil Registration Act 2004. This Act states that changes will be made to the rules relating to who can solemnise a marriage, where marriages can take place, and how marriages are registered. Civil marriage ceremonies will no longer be confined to registry offices. With the agreement of the person conducting the wedding you will be able to get married in a much wider variety of places, including hotels, parks and public places, subject to certain conditions. 'Suitability' is one such condition, and relates to how well the location reflects the solemnity of the occasion. For the latest news on the reform, see *groireland.ie*.

Exchange of rings If you are having a registry wedding you don't have to do the exchange of rings there. You can save the ring exchanging ceremony till later, perhaps when all your guests are assembled before the first dance.

Eco-Ethical Eye

Candles for Peace The Benedictine monks of Rostrevor in Co. Antrim make candles for peace and reconciliation. Following the rules of St Benedict, the monks support themselves by making handicrafts. Using only the best materials, they produce these high quality decorative candles. They have a wide range of decorations: hand-painted candles, candles adorned with designs of appliqué wax and others using dried flowers. Their particular mission is to contribute to reconciliation between Catholics and Protestants. I had these reasonably priced candles at my wedding and I can highly recommend the service. Allow good time for orders. (See *benedictinemonks.co.uk/handicraft/*.)

Confetti Be sure to use the biodegradable variety. Not only is it more environmentally friendly but it is the only confetti allowed by many celebrants. (See *confettidirect.co.uk*.) You could also collect rose petals that your local florist will be throwing out. White feathers are also an option and they look great in photographs, especially for that kissing shot outside the church! Don't throw rice though, as this is harmful to birds.

Potted plants Cut flowers are often flown long distances to Ireland, causing unnecessary carbon emissions. Purchasing beautiful potted plants or trees to decorate the entrance of your ceremony space not only reduces waste but you can continue to enjoy them on your patio for many months. Planting the trees will also offset some of the carbon emissions caused by your wedding! Marks & Spencer sell some really elaborate potted plants that will definitely create a wow factor. You could complement these plants with cheaper white plants from your local garden centre.

 WARNING

Children We have all been there . . . just as the beaming groom is slipping the ring on the bride's trembling finger to the gentle strumming of a guitar, lo and behold, there is always one toddler right up front banging Mammy's Ray-Bans across the back of the seat. Despite all eyes burning into the back of the parents they are blissfully unaware that their child is (a) annoying the bride and groom during the most important moment of the day, (b) ruining the atmosphere, and (c) breaking the videographer's heart for sound quality reasons and finally, (d) the child will probably never receive a birthday card from the couple again! So, gently ask *in advance* of the ceremony that children are taken out if making noise.

Priests Servants of the Lord, yes. But not *your* servant! The normal church for a wedding is in the parish of the bride, but a couple can approach any Catholic priest and request permission to be married in a church of their choice. It is good to remember that a priest in such a parish is under no obligation to facilitate you. Most parishes where weddings are popular will ask the couple to provide their own priest.

Try to work with the priest when choosing your readings and music. If you want to go down the aisle to Greenday you might want to run it by the priest in time to arrange something new. Many singers will draw the line at certain songs in a church, which is beyond your control. It is *your* day, yes, but if your priest will not budge when it comes to allowing non-religious music you will still have all evening to play whatever you like. Or you could meet half-way with an instrumental.

Mobiles will ring unless you ask the priest to suggest all mobiles be turned off. The priest who married myself and my husband has a good trick of starting off welcoming people: 'You have all rushed here today, getting ready in the morning, probably trying to follow directions to the church, getting seated, *turning off your mobiles* . . . and now we are all settled and it is time to relax and enjoy the day.' This worked a treat. If your priest does not want to do this, you could ask a friend to simply ring a mobile before the bride arrives; this usually reminds people to check their phones.

Quiet At our rehearsal my priest commented that it is important that the bridal party try to keep the following in mind. When guests start to arrive at the church, if there is furious chatter between the bridal party, checking watches, talking on mobiles inside the church, parents running back and forth to the car, this sets the tone, and some guests will become chatty and the noise levels will rise. A wedding is a solemn event and calm and whispered voices from the bridal party will set the respectful tone appropriate to the church or registry. Ask a musician to play some gentle music before the start time.

Webguide

benedictinemonks.co.uk The Benedictine Monks (candles)
citizensinformation.ie
confettidirect.co.uk Wedding shop
gettingmarried.ie Catholic Ireland guide to getting married
groni.gov.uk The General Register Office, Northern Ireland
groireland.ie The General Register Office, Ireland
irish-humanists.org Humanist Association of Ireland
myweddingbox.co.uk Wedding shop
reasonableribbon.com Cheap ribbon shop
webwedding.co.uk Wedding shop (listen to wedding music online resource)
xena-productions.com Wedding planner and hire service

Chapter Four

The Reception Venue

Whether you have a buffet, a five-course meal, a garden party or a céilí, you will need a venue. This chapter will look at how your choice of venue and the decisions you make about your reception can have a very positive impact on your budget.

⁂ First Decisions

Weigh up what matters to you most. Within even the smallest budget you should be able to find somewhere offering, at the very least, good food, a comfortable environment and efficient staff. You may want a venue you can bring your own wine to, perhaps a nicely decorated room, or a room with a view, or a discount on rooms for your guests. When considering your priorities, bear in mind that the average guest will tell you that what matters most to them is a nice tasty dinner served on time with some good wine in comfortable surroundings. Beautiful scenery, fancy chandeliers, even the choice of music is often much less important to your guests than good food. So for the sake of a good party and happy memories all round, this decision should be given time and research.

 WARNING

No amount of scenery and high ceilings will compensate for slow service and salty soup.

Research Searching for your venue will probably start at your computer. To find contact details and web addresses of some great venues and unusual rooms for hire, visit *venuesearch.ie*. From pubs, restaurants and hotels through to castles and historical buildings, this website has them all. You simply enter your ideal type of venue, the number of guests you expect and your preferred location and, hey presto, it throws up your options. Priceless.

Georgina Campbell's book *Ireland for Romantic Weddings and Honeymoons* is an excellent reference guide full of dream venues, many of them at not unreasonable prices. See the interview with Georgina on page 38. You can also do your own search on Georgina's website *ireland-guide.com*.

Of course, word of mouth is always invaluable. For marketing-free reviews ask people you know and trust about their experience of weddings in the past. Probe as many people as you can for information about the venues you have in mind. Did you like the food? Was the service good? No brochure or wedding magazine will tell you if the hotel function room is always baking in July due to lack of air conditioning, or that the service was so slow the meal didn't end till ten. These are things that are essential to know.

What type of venue? For large weddings, hotels and castles are the most popular choice. Another popular choice is renting a hall or function room and arranging the event through caterers. The fewer guests you have, the broader your choice of venue. Some smaller, more exclusive restaurants with additional function rooms are perfect for intimate weddings.

Hotel Some couples start out adamant that they don't want a *hotel* wedding, but when they start to realise the major organisation involved in holding an event for 150 people, the positives in going with a hotel start to shine through. There are so many fantastic hotels in Ireland you will not be stuck for choice. A good hotel will come with professional and efficient staff to manage and oversee your event. For larger weddings, as well as being the easier choice, a hotel is often the most economical choice. The cost will depend largely on your choice of menu. If you are not interested in a large hotel, why not look at some of the small boutique hotels which can be very 'un-hotely' in their intimate surroundings.

Castles Believe it or not, castles don't always cost more than hotels. So why not aim high? Remember, as with a hotel, only go with a castle if you know they can deliver. You might get the 'medieval look' you are after but if your guests are uncomfortable in a draughty room waiting for the meal, or the meal itself tastes nothing near as grand as the surroundings, you might have made the wrong decision. Be careful what you dream of . . .

fairytale surroundings are one thing, a good meal and a great party are another! The same applies to all venues.

> **The Rectory, Glandore, West Cork**
> In one of Ireland's most beautiful sea inlets, this early nineteenth-century residence is nestled amidst wooded hills overlooking the scenic West Cork harbour. The Georgian restaurant with its huge bay windows serves first-class gourmet food in this perfect location for a wedding of up to 100. (See *rectoryglandore.com*.)

Restaurants Booking your favourite restaurant for the evening is a lovely option for the smaller wedding. Most restaurants will facilitate weddings. Discuss minimum spend to cover them closing for the day.

Country Houses If you want something different, off the beaten track, a country house might be for you. The standard of food, wine and surroundings is usually very high. It is not always the cheaper option but if you keep the numbers down it is often achievable on a small budget. You can let your imagination run wild in these locations, with wholesome food, fine wines, regal surroundings. Visit *hiddenireland.ie* or *ireland-guide.com* for many hidden gems.

> **Crypt Wedding?**
> Celebrate in the largest crypt in Ireland in Christchurch Cathedral. This was previously used as a market place in medieval times and now houses an exhibition of church treasures. (See *cccdub.ie*.)

First Steps

Make contact Call or email your favourite venues requesting a brochure before you visit. When assessing the cost of a venue it is not simply price per head, it is about the package the hotel is willing to offer you. Remember that what is written in the brochure is always negotiable.

Bargain Don't be shy about looking for a better deal. The person you meet will inevitably open out a well-scribbled diary on the table in front of you, tell you they are booked up till 2010 but will see if they can 'fit you in'. Don't be put off by this. Use the 'dream' card. Insist that this is where you have wanted your wedding for years but you just can't go with the prices on offer. Try to win them over: lay it on thick, get out the violins if you have to; no one needs to know that you are negotiating with three other venues. If the venue still doesn't budge and you have really fallen in love with the place above any other, maybe with some cutbacks in other areas or using imaginative alternatives you can save enough to have your wedding in your ideal venue.

Cash Register

As Eddie Hobbs says, these days many guests give cash gifts. The average gift from a couple is between €100 and €150. Don't rely on this as there will be those who purchase a gift or don't give a gift, but it is comforting to know that there will be a certain cushion provided from the cash you do receive. If you have qualms about asking for cash (or if you think it is vulgar) then you can spread the word with a small number of close friends or relatives. And if you don't set up a registry list, then the hint should be well and truly received.

Get the rock bottom price It is best to discuss it all at the outset and be clear on what you plan to spend. Before deciding on anywhere, you need to ask a lot of questions. This will help you decide by having a good idea of the minimum spend you can get away with for each venue.

Questions for your venue

- What time of the year can you offer me the best deal?
- Do you do a weekday discount?
- Do you have a minimum number for guests?
- What is the price per head for a standard meal?
- What is the price per head for late evening food?
- Can I serve my own wine? What is the corkage?
- If not, what sort of a deal can you offer me on the wine?
- Can I serve cake as dessert?
- Can I decide on my own menu?
- How is the room decorated? Physically call to the venue to see the room dressed prior to a wedding. It may not be the same as pictured in the brochure (mine was better, which sealed the deal!).
- Do the bride and groom get a night in the hotel for free? (If not, this is very unusual and very tight.)

- Will there be a free tea/coffee reception for guests?
- Is it child-friendly?
- Is it wheelchair accessible?
- Package add-ons to seal the deal — can your florist decorate my cake while doing the tables? Can you offer discounted room rates for guests?
- How many weddings do you cater for per day?
- Which entrance will I be using?
- Any building work planned/scheduled? If so, how does it impact on the hotel?
- Will the lobby be presentable for guests? (I once had lunch in a hotel where I noticed a wedding party was gathered for pre-dinner drinks in the lobby. Above them hung a large red plastic banner advertising 'Special Offer Wedding Packages' in gaudy white print. It just looked terrible!)
- Are there bedrooms directly over the function and if so, how long can my music continue?
- How long will the bar be open? If it closes at 12.30, how much to keep it open another hour?

> **How to sour an evening?**
> One newlywed recently complained on a message board that the hotel manager asked the groom to settle the bill on the night of the wedding!

⏱ Good Timing

Time of year As I said above, when you are choosing between venues be sure to ask them when they would be able to offer you their cheapest rate. It is well known that there are very quiet months on the wedding calendar so they should be glad of some business and should offer you a discount at those times.

Midweek offers If you are having your reception on a weekday (Monday to Thursday), expect to receive a 10% discount on menu prices from the hotel, which is becoming very much industry standard — although you can push for more. You will need to factor in that people will have to take more time off if it is, say, a Tuesday or Wednesday. If you have guests travelling long distances, a midweek wedding could seriously eat into their annual leave. However, a Monday wedding or a Thursday are very popular choices.

Seasonal decorations If you are having a Christmas wedding, be sure to check when the decorations go up. Similarly, if you are having a wedding around Halloween, you might not be happy to see fake cobwebs and plastic spider webs all over the lobby.

◐ Something Different

Outdoor party Using a parent's garden, or your own, and sourcing your own catering might be an option for you. Some couples, for more relaxed weddings, are happy to rely on some gazebos from Dunnes Stores or Lidl, and hope for the best weatherwise. This is only possible if the house or a nearby pub is suitable as a back-up location.

Marquee To be a little safer you would need to arrange a marquee. Marquee weddings can be absolutely beautiful, you have so much scope to decorate the wedding the way you want. You can have one main marquee or a few little mini marquees scattered about the garden. Some couples even have hay bails brought on to the green area for guests to sit on with a bonfire and candles in glass lanterns hanging from trees! It is certainly a way to be creative. But be prepared for the end of day bill to be similar or higher than that of a very good hotel wedding. The organisation involved can also triple when sourcing your own caterers, toilets, alcohol. To see how a marquee can look in photographs and get a feel for what you will pay, visit *marquee.ie* or *weddingsathome.ie*. Weddings At Home, who offer a wedding package deal, cutting out a good bit of organisation, advise that for a 150-person wedding package you will pay €16,500 (Mon–Fri) and €16,875 (Sat–Sun), which works out at approximately €110 per head. You will get a White Lined Marquee with hard floor, tables, chairs, crockery, cutlery, linen, glassware, flowers, Pimm's reception, extensive menu, entertainment, staff and midnight BBQ. You will need then to supply wine for the meal or request the caterer to do this. Further arrangements will also be needed such as toilet facilities and bar facilities. If it is a spring or autumn wedding, heating requirements may need to be put in place. Later in the evening you cannot have a cash bar unless you apply for a temporary license to serve alcohol. So you will probably need to have enough wine for the day. Separating out the marquee hire, catering and entertainment could bring the end total down, but you will need to do considerable research as prices can vary from €4,000 to €9,000 for marquee rental alone. You will then have to source the tables and chairs, flooring, lighting etc, often from the same rental company but at extra cost. So, a marquee wedding may not be as economical as you'd imagine. There is also the option of having a marquee wedding *at* a hotel. Coolbawn Quay in Tipperary, for example, specialise in marquee weddings. This is a very unique location and it will still work out expensive. You may be charged a rental fee to put a marquee on the site and then pay a price per head for food and wine. Some country homes may do a deal allowing you to use the lawn if they cater the event.

> We wanted a relatively short engagement and six months was as quick as we could manage. It focuses the mind and does not allow the wedding process take over your life. The venue is the normal immediate question but the way we got around that was having a marquee, so our immediate question was caterer and church availability.
>
> Having a marquee presents a different set of issues to plan for (the guests tend to go straight from the church to the reception when they're going to a marquee, sometimes with a hotel reception guests can tend to wander before they arrive at the reception).
>
> We also needed a solution to the midnight sandwiches supply. Again, when you're not in a hotel you need to be a bit more resourceful. Our solution was to hire a chip-van, we all know how good a burger and chips taste at that time in the evening!
>
> **Ruth and Ultan, Sligo**

Boat club, tennis club, golf club? Are you or your partner, or either of your parents affiliated with any club, organisation or even college? They may offer you a venue at a reduced cost.

Castle with Cobwebs — For a very small wedding (16)

'The impact of this rare and authentic castle's historic appeal and significance is literally instant — as if having just stepped from a time machine you will be overwhelmed by an immediate sense of having been transported back in time through turbulent centuries of history. Six-feet thick battle-impenetrable walls, winding spiral stone staircase, oak-beamed ceilings and flagstone floors will offer you this once-in-a-lifetime opportunity to experience how they lived back in 1420.'

Fifteenth-century Irish castle in Co. Clare, completely intact and furnished with antiques to maintain its olde-world charm and, oh yes, cobwebs! (See *ballyhannon-castle.com*.)

 # Clever Tips

Hotels will often have more than one function room, as well as conference and board rooms for hire. If you plan a smaller, more casual event — perhaps a wine and cheese evening for a few people — remember this.

We used a sailing club as the venue and hired a caterer to do a carvery-style hot buffet. We hired chairs, tables, and decorated it ourselves with stenciled muslin, gold-sprayed seashells, ivy, for sea theme. We had a fabulous jazz singer with pianist for about a third the cost of a band, and she was much, much better.

Vanya, Dublin

 # Webguide

ballyhannon-castle.com   *irishgems.com*
cccdub.ie   *irishluxury.com*
goireland.com   *marquee.ie*
hiddenireland.com   *rectoryglandore.com*
inishboffin.com   *venuesearch.ie*
ireland-guide.com   *weddingsathome.ie*
irelandsbluebook.com

✻   ✻   ✻

Georgina Campbell on Romantic Weddings and Honeymoons

Author and commentator on quality in Ireland for over twenty years, Georgina Campbell talks about the motivations and criteria used when compiling her list of the best: *Georgina Campbell's Ireland for Romantic Weddings and Honeymoons:*

All of our selected wedding venues are special, but **value is to be found in some unexpected places:** prices can be deceptive — a superficially attractive price could be compromised by a long list of extras, for example — so get out your calculator and work out the real cost per head, as you could be pleasantly surprised.

That indefinable special something Over and above the usual criteria for our guides (high standards of accommodation, food and service, at a fair price) the key requirement for *Romantic Weddings* was that venues selected should have an indefinable special something that set them apart from more ordinary places. In marketing terms I suppose this would be called a 'unique selling point'; it's to do with being romantic rather than necessarily luxurious.

The most important thing to get right I'd say is the venue and then tailor other things — numbers, the date — around that. Once you've found the right place — and this means not only the perfect venue but the people that you feel you can trust absolutely with the responsibility of running your big day — everything else will gradually fall into place.

A most important point about prices/value — look very carefully at prices, as the more expensive-looking ones may work out better value for money when you analyse what you get (i.e. a better service and less extra expenses).

I think people get far too hung up about numbers — i.e. being obliged to have a big wedding in order to fit in all the people who 'have' to be invited (there were only seventeen of us at my own wedding, at the Roundwood Inn, a decade or three ago!)

The day of the week. A Saturday is admittedly most considerate for people who have to take time off work, but guests are generally prepared to fit in.

Working out the accommodation logistics is important too, for everybody's relaxation during the event; on-site accommodation is by far the best option — especially where there are elderly guests who may need to take a quiet break during the day, or parents with young children who may need attention; having guests spread around a large area can be nerve-wracking — and busing people can be a nightmare too. So a venue that has room for everyone to stay, with other options nearby (e.g. inexpensive B&B accommodation) is ideal. Where the wedding is local to most of the guests, a restaurant can be a good choice (best of all, a restaurant with rooms).

Then there is good food — a basic requirement when making the choice of venue, but selecting the menu carefully to suit the numbers makes a big difference too; best to avoid things like roasts that get 'tired' easily, for example. Testing the actual menu selected is important, and many venues offer it as part of the package.

Something a lot of couples don't give a lot of thought to is the sound system — and, especially, the volume of music. People attending weddings are often trying to get to know other guests — new in-laws and their friends — or meeting old friends/relatives they haven't seen for ages and it's really frustrating to be unable to have conversations after the meal.

If you are looking for a 'different' venue, there are lots of unusual venues in *Romantic Weddings* — castles are always a winner for atmosphere, and they can be surprisingly good value too. If you work out what you actually get for the money at Lismore Castle, for example, it's remarkably good value. Coolbawn Quay in Co. Tipperary is a very unusual waterside venue — there are plenty of others in the book.

Honeymooning in Ireland. Firstly, it's a wonderfully romantic country once you get away from your workaday situation and it's amazing how few people living in Ireland know the country well. No need for all the stress of airports, detailed itineraries, multiple changes of outfits for different climates and goodness knows what — just choose one or more of our fabulously romantic spots (two or three days in each is about right, unless you're very sure you want to stay in one place) and you wouldn't want to be anywhere else — Donegal, Mayo, Galway, Kerry, west Waterford — and more. So many beautiful, still unspoilt places to find real relaxation after all the pre-wedding stress. Plenty of ideas in the book!

Throwing a Party

Chapter Five

Food

Food is an essential part of any celebration. For a guest, the typical wedding day is long, often starting with a rush in the morning to get ready, travel to the ceremony and onwards to the hotel. This all takes time and by late afternoon most guests are very hungry and ready for some good food. Even if it is finger food at an evening party it should be given a lot of consideration. Tasty food does not have to cost the earth and can be found in the plainest looking venues. Remember, you can dress up a room but you can't dress up bad food. A recent trend in banqueting is a return to simple dishes made with good local ingredients. This is great news for anyone on a budget, as simpler, less labour-intensive dishes allow you to serve high-quality, tasty food at a reasonable cost.

✴ First Decisions

Tea and coffee on arrival Most guests arrive at the venue craving a cup of tea and a small bite. Anyone on a tight budget should really by-pass the idea of a drinks reception, which I will discuss further in Chapter Six. Guests will have been chatting after the ceremony and may have lost your directions and taken a wrong turn on the way, so you can be guaranteed they will be (a) gasping for a cuppa and (b) starving. If you listen closely you will hear this whispered in the lobby at most weddings. So, why not add something a little more substantial to the biscuits at your tea and coffee reception? You could surprise your guests with some fruit scones, muffins or fairy cakes. It is a lovely personal touch. Also, try to avoid delay in arriving yourself and insist your hotel serve the meal on time. These are small details that can make the day much more comfortable for your guests.

A sit-down meal Most weddings involve a sit-down four- or five-course meal. Variations which are becoming more popular include a buffet, a barbeque, or a meal in a restaurant. Food is usually priced 'per head'. Caterers also tend to price food 'per head'. For a buffet you can usually get away with rounding down, assuming not everyone will eat the same amount. Price per head is an important figure but remember to look at the whole package when comparing venues. Extra food, such as offering a second choice of main or starter, will add to the price. All good venues should have a vegetarian option and, given notice, will cater for special diets. Expect to pay between €30 and €80 (of course it can go higher!) in most hotels. Add approximately €5 per head if you decide to include a choice.

Buffet Having a buffet instead of a five-course meal can look very elegant and offer more choice to guests while sometimes costing less than a sit-down meal. The food can be as simple as a selection of cold meats, salads and savouries with breads, or as hearty as a hot carvery with vegetables and all the trimmings. It has another advantage in that guests will circulate during the meal, allowing more interaction between tables. For a summer wedding a buffet is ideal, as food tends to be lighter and people often don't eat as much as they might in winter. Choosing a buffet can also make the day that little bit different.

There are various options as to how to run the buffet, the most economical being to serve the starter at the table and then allow guests to go to a serving station for their mains and to finish with the cake served as dessert. It is generally recommended that you have a staff member attend the food stations, as hungry people tend to take more than they can eat. Some hotels require a minimum of 50–100 people before they will accept a buffet booking.

☺ Self-sufficient

Okay, there is being self-sufficient and then there is madness . . . even Nigella Lawson or Gordon Ramsay wouldn't cook their own wedding feast, so I am not going to suggest it. But there are some nice touches you can arrange yourself.

Afternoon tea As I said, it is nice to offer guests something more substantial than a biscuit when they arrive at the venue. You could easily bake this yourself or ask a family member to do it and freeze it ready to be taken out the day before the wedding. This was something my hotel had no problem with me doing. I ordered Bakewell tarts and scones from my local bakery, and some Scottish guests we had came armed with shortbread, which the staff kindly arranged for my guests. For an extra special touch you could arrange with your venue to include some pots of jam and clotted cream. This won't ruin anyone's appetite but it will tide over the hungriest guests until the food is served. My guests certainly appreciated this; in fact, the plates were empty by the time I arrived!

☀ Clever Tips

Food at weddings can get overwhelming for guests if there are too many courses or very heavy dishes combined. Choose wholesome, tasty food that doesn't cost too much and you can redirect your savings there into some late evening food. You can mix and match the sample menus. Chat to the hotel staff about your decisions; they will most likely know the crowd-pleasing dishes and how to combine foods well. Keep the following in mind ...

Taste the food If your venue does not do a menu tasting, eat in their restaurant where you should be able to get a feel for the standard. You could also suggest visiting while they are holding another wedding and ask for a side plate portion of the dishes being served.

Local foods in season should be cheaper so pinpoint the items that cost less and you can probably see why.

Starter vs soup There is also a great saving if you serve either a starter *or* a soup. You don't need to have the two.

Skip the choice Having a set main rather than a choice can save you about €5 per head. If you choose something universally popular, such as lamb, beef or chicken, the minority that want something different can be catered for with the vegetarian option or your hotel might provide a fish option. This is something that many people do these days; it is an economical choice and it also saves on waste — so much food at weddings goes into the bin.

Easy peasy If you are going with a plated starter, choose something which is less labour intensive. It is probably cheaper as a result.

Serving the cake as dessert is a popular option. It is just as suitable a dessert as an apple pie or brownie. It will reduce the price per head and so allows you to spend a little more on a really impressive cake if you like. If you are worried your cake won't cover everyone for dessert, you can order a large undecorated sheet cake for the kitchen to divide out. Georgina Campbell's book *Romantic Weddings and Honeymoons* highlights which venues allow you to do this.

Speeches If you think your speeches are going to be long, consider starting them a little earlier, when dessert is served. Or borrow the American idea of having the first two speeches in between courses. This is an import that is gaining popularity in Ireland.

🕐 Good Timing

Seasonal feasts On page 49 you will find a table listing fruits, vegetables and meats in season around the time of your wedding. Themes incorporating food offer up so many possibilities. For a winter wedding greet your guests with mulled wine and mince pies. A hearty soup can do as the main starter, warming your guests up on a snowy day. The traditional ham and turkey meal is always a winner, especially around Christmas, and this dish usually costs less too. Christmas cake can be bought in the shops and used as the wedding cake. It is even better if you are having a January wedding — with all the special offers on Christmas cake you won't need to look far!

In spring, you can decorate the tables with daisy rings, painted eggs and gingham tablecloths. Around Easter you could brighten up your guests' chairs with colourful bows and assorted mini eggs as edible favours. Chilled fruit juices served with cheese and grapes on crackers can greet your guests on a hot summer's afternoon. Autumn with its golden leaves falling from the trees, allows you go rustic with rich colours: browns and greens with clove-studded oranges to decorate the centre of the tables.

If you are going with a seasonal food theme, a thoughtful gesture would be to print the recipe of what your guests are eating to leave on the tables. Chat to your chef about how the meal was put together and your guests can enjoy recreating the tastes at home.

The possibilities are endless.

❶ Something Different

For a smaller wedding a **barbeque** is a lovely idea, particularly for anyone having a garden party after the ceremony. Rent a marquee and hire staff to organise the food. With Irish weather be sure to have a back-up room indoors. For more on marquees see Chapter Three.

Skip dinner and have a party By asking guests to attend an evening celebration you can be sure some of them will be pleased. Weddings are special, enjoyable events but many people see them as hard work, between getting dressed up, arranging accommodation, finding the church, finding the hotel, waiting for the meal and chatting to people all day. There is no denying it can make some people wedding weary. A crowd-pleasing alternative is an intimate ceremony and meal followed by a larger evening party that everyone will enjoy. You could even video the ceremony and play back the vows to your evening guests.

Cocktail party With the savings you make from keeping most of the day small you could splash out on an impressive venue, nice finger food, even a cocktail reception with a jazz band! Invite the guests to your 'Wedding Cocktail Party'. It will give your female guests an excuse to buy a sexy cocktail dress! This is a particularly good idea for those getting married in a tropical location, as the possibilities for 'theming' things up are endless.

Dessert wedding This quirky American idea is the stuff that dreams are made of! An evening party, with that little bit extra in the form of dessert heaven. Alongside some savoury finger food, the idea is to have a table (or trolleys!) of mouth-watering desserts, bowls of fruit, some fruit punch and/or cookie cocktails. This is different, exciting and tasty all in one. You could even send out some fudge with your invitations, to give your guests a taste of what's to come!

Eco-Ethical Eye

Choosing locally grown, seasonal produce will have a significant, positive impact upon the local economy. Whether you are putting on your own banquet or leaving food and drink to the experts in your chosen venue, ask them if they can source locally and organically where possible. Buying seasonally helps negate the need for artificial heating in glasshouses. If you are buying organic food, remember to buy locally grown organic food rather than imported. To give an idea of how far food travels, a typical basket of 26 imported organic foods may have travelled the distance of six times around the equator!

Avoid waste If you have decided on a choice for your main course, simply putting 'Beef or Salmon' under the 'will/will not be attending' line on an RSVP can save you money. This is something many couples do and you should not hesitate in doing it. Letting your venue know in advance of the exact quantities required should save you money but it will definitely save on a massive amount of waste in the kitchen. Be sure to colour code your place names so the waiting staff know who wants what, because your guests may forget!

Eco theme Food lovers can choose an organic or local theme for their wedding. For a larger wedding, with current prices, an organic menu would most likely cost more than the average price per head. However, choosing to serve a local menu should work out cheaper. Let your guests know on the menu what comes from where (on recycled paper of course!). You could add a short paragraph on why you chose to serve local food, who knows, you might inspire others to try their own local farmers' market, or even just to think about how they shop and the impact it has on the environment.

January
scallops
pears
turnips
carrots
goose
leeks
squash
cabbage
parsnips
shallots
lobster
forced rhubarb
celeriac

February
goose
halibut
guinea fowl
leeks
squash
cabbage
parsnips
shallots
lobster
forced rhubarb
celeriac
mussels
cabbage
chicory

March
early rhubarb
radishes
rhubarb
sardines
carrots
leeks
purple-sprouting
    broccoli
lobster
sorrel
beetroot
mint

April
rosemary
spinach
spring lamb
strawberries
cockles
morel mushrooms
wild garlic
radishes
rhubarb
carrots
kale
watercress

May
samphire
duck
sea trout
asparagus
cherries
cauliflower
new potatoes
sea bass
raspberries
parsley
mint
broad beans
lemon sole
sardines
rhubarb
new carrots
strawberries

June
grey mullet
gooseberries
tayberries
courgettes
broad beans
Welsh lamb
elderflowers
lettuce
crab
strawberries
peppers
asparagus
redcurrants
salmon
cherries
aubergines
peas

July
blueberries
clams
pike
aubergines
fennel
tomatoes
strawberries
trout
watercress
pilchards
loganberries
sage
cauliflower
raspberries

August
greengages
crayfish
hare
basil
peas
lettuce
john dory
fennel
aubergines
peppers
courgettes
strawberries
sweetcorn

September
damsons and plums
blackberries
sweetcorn
autumn lamb
apples
partridge
brown trout
duck
venison
cucumbers
spinach
figs
grouse
mussels
sea bass
onions

October
autumn lamb
elderberries
figs
grouse
oysters
guinea fowl
squash
beetroot
mushrooms
courgettes
marrow
partridge
mussels
apples
kale
pumpkin

November
parsnips
chestnuts
beetroot
goose
cranberries
grouse
swede
cabbage
potatoes
teal
pumpkins
pears
leeks
quinces

December
sea bass
turkey
pomegranate
celery
red cabbage
wild duck
swede
celeriac
turnips
sprouts
goose
pumpkins
beetroot
parsnips
pears

Source: *bbc.co.uk/food*

Webguide

bbc.co.uk/food This site is so simple to follow and discusses everything from food basics — such as foods in season (see table), what goes well together, recipes through to celebrity chefs and their creations. You can take the Masterchef course online if you are really serious about learning more about food for your wedding!

odlums.ie For recipe ideas.

tasteofireland.com Wine and food expert Paolo Tullio's website with restaurant and food reviews, details of farmers' markets and wine pages.

Chapter Six

Champagne, Buck's Fizz and Wine

At your wedding you will be expected to provide wine for your guests with their meal. In Ireland this is an important gesture and no matter how small your budget I would not recommend skipping it! If you choose a good wine and provide a glass and a half or two for each guest you have more than covered the drinks aspect of your wedding. Those looking for more are never far from a bar.

🎇 First Decisions

Some couples choose to have a formal drinks reception on arrival, a toast drink or an open bar (one drink per guest). You will need to go through these options and decide if this is somewhere you want to spend or save.

Drinks on guests' arrival Tea and coffee are often supplied free of charge by hotels. I didn't bother with drinks on arrival myself, the option would have cost me more than my flower budget and as a waitress at many weddings in the past I knew that half the bubbles go down the sink! A hotel manager I spoke with recently commented that he feels the drinks reception is often wasted money. With most hotels having a bar in the lobby, a tea and coffee reception often hits the spot for guests after the ceremony and drive from the church. Many men prefer a pint and women a pre-dinner gin and tonic. A wine reception on top of wine at the tables is often excessive. If you want some bubbles at the reception why not save it for a traditional champagne toast.

Wine with the meal Two glasses per guest or one glass followed by a top-up is the usual serving during the main meal at a wedding. You might want to factor in another top-up for when the speeches start, as a 'toast' drink. One bottle will provide five standard glasses of wine. At a table of ten, allowing for two glasses each, you will only need four bottles. If you instruct staff to only open the bottles required, then you will save on waste. This is especially important if you bring your own wine to the venue.

Toast Here it is usual to either top up the wine or offer a different drink. When on a tight budget, topping up the wine is perfect. Believe me, guests have full bellies, and are tucking into their dessert. There will be a full glass of wine next to them and probably tea and coffee being served. Whether another drink is served at this point will not matter to them. Because some bubbles was something I wanted, I served a small glass of sparkling wine for each guest at this point. In my view the 'open bar' option is budget-destroying madness. With drinks prices in Ireland at the moment this is an extremely expensive gesture. Since my wedding I have attended four weddings where there was no toast drink, which I did not even notice until I started researching this chapter.

☀ Clever Tips

Service Having staff serving the wine not only looks very professional but means you will have more control. Leaving bottles on the table usually allows people to help themselves to more and so the wine runs out sooner. What also happens is bottles are opened towards the end of the meal that are not finished. If this is the case be sure to instruct the staff to leave the wine on a table in the corner for guests to continue to enjoy.

Purchase the **house wine** in your venue. Unless wine is 'your thing', it is safer, and cheaper, to go with the house wine, which is usually tried and trusted. Your wedding day is not the day to experiment unless you or a friend knows what to look for. Speak to the manager or the sommelier for advice.

Fizz tips If you do go with a champagne reception or champagne toast, keep the following in mind. Everyone enjoys the quality of champagne but still wonders why there is such a difference in price between still wines and fizzy. The title of this book is *How to Have a Champagne Wedding on a Buck's Fizz Budget* because you *can* have a brilliant wedding without spending a bomb, just as you can have a really tasty glass of bubbly without spending champagne prices. Tesco has proved that champagne producers can get a world-class product to market at a lower price. In 2004 Tesco's own label champagne, Premier Cru Champagne, one of the cheapest in Ireland and Britain at €26.49, beat 282 other more expensive brands — Taittinger, Lanson, Mumm — in a blind tasting test to win a top award (the Non-vintage Champagne Trophy) at the International Wine Challenge in London. The moral of the story — serve sparkling wine, no one will know the difference.

> Make your bubbles go longer: half bubbles, half orange juice — our favourite, **Buck's Fizz,** refreshing with a little kick!

☺ Self-sufficient

BYO Bring your own. If your wedding is in a hotel or castle you will probably have to pay corkage. So be sure to check if it is worth your while. A saving of €2 per bottle is worth your while if you are serving 100 bottles on the day. Corkage prices will range from €4 to €20 and corkage for wine is not always the same as for champagne. Another reason to skip champagne!

Where?

France You are allowed to buy 90 litres of wine, which is 120 bottles. Irish Ferries do an eight-hour trip, Rosslare to Cherbourg. Brittany Ferries have something similar from Cork to Roscoff. If you do go, bring proof that it is all for consumption on your wedding day at the venue, just in case you are asked. You could take your notice of marriage papers and a few invitations to show the officials if they ask. Many supermarkets are literally outside the tunnel so you won't have to travel far!

Up North Wine is often cheaper in Northern Ireland. Many couples make a trip to Newry, for example, to load up the car for Christmas. During sales times this can work out even cheaper. Supermarkets such as Sainsbury's do excellent offers.

Supermarkets Tesco, Marks & Spencer, Superquinn — be prepared to pounce when these supermarkets announce their special offers. You might want to stay in the long grass for a while to see who has the best offers but when you spot a really good deal go for it.

Off-Licences O'Briens, Oddbins — Sign up for newsletters or join mailing lists at wine shops. Then, when wines you want for your wedding go on sale, you can buy in bulk.

Most merchants offer a **10 percent discount** for buying wine by the case, and they'll often increase that if you purchase several cases at once.

Check into wine that's **available in magnums** (bottles double the size of regular ones); several quality wines are. Wine sold in a magnum costs less per ounce, and because the corkage fee goes twice as far, you'll save on two counts. Check first with your hotel as some may charge extra corkage.

Or you could **try an importer**, such as *mywine.ie* in Cork, to select wines for you. 'My Wine' specially chooses varieties from independent wine producers from famous French wine regions operating both as a wholesaler and retailer. They can deliver direct to your door within 48 hours of purchase to anywhere in Ireland or Northern Ireland (subject to stock).

> If bringing your own wine, ask that the left-over bottles are stored for you. If you have any guests staying on a second night, they can enjoy them with dinner the following evening.

Good Timing

Sales As I said above, don't underestimate the saving that can be made by waiting for sales. Don't be afraid to phone around looking for sales times. It is not unheard of to save up to €15 off the normal price of champagne during sales.

 Eco-Ethical Eye

Carbon emissions It may be cheaper in monetary terms to buzz across to France and buy your own wine, but how much is this trip costing the planet? Take the hassle out of your own hands and liaise with a local supplier; or ask the hotel to arrange the wine.

Recycle Make sure you recycle all that glass! If the venue does not recycle, it's about time somebody asked them why.

Stay local You can have wines produced in England delivered to a Northern Irish address. Try *englishwineproducers.com* or *english-wine.com* for English and Welsh vineyards.

Ordering fair-trade You can download lists of fair-trade certified wines, spirits, beers and ale at *fairtrade.org.uk* or *traidcraft.co.uk*. These companies will only ship to Northern Ireland.

Webguide

fairtrade.org.uk
mywine.ie Wine importer
thewineroom.ie Wine shop and discussion
traidcraft.co.uk
wineandbeerworld.com British wine merchant in France. You must pre-order rather than just arrive at their premises.

Paolo Tullio on Choosing Your Wine

Author, critic, actor and broadcaster Paulo Tullio is the host and the author of *tasteofireland.com*, a website dedicated to the joys of food and wine. He is the restaurant reviewer and wine correspondent for the *Irish Independent* and also contributes articles on lifestyle and travel. Paolo is also a regular contributor to *Food & Wine* magazine.

For people who know very little about wine, where would you point them?

Paolo If you're not confident enough in your own judgement, don't buy in supermarkets; go to where you can get advice, like a well-established wine merchant. You'll pay a little more, but you won't end up with an embarrassingly bad choice.

When choosing a wine for your wedding, how do you pick something which will please everyone and yet still avoid a wine lacking character?

Paolo I don't think you can do both. A wine with character is like someone with a big extrovert personality, it will please some people and get right up the noses of others. The trick when trying to please a lot of people is to pick a wine whose characteristics are restrained. That doesn't necessarily mean 'lacking in character', just that their attributes aren't screamingly loud. Avoid wines with pronounced characteristics — anything made from the Muscat grape, big Aussie Shiraz, flabby Chilean Merlot, Gewurztraminer or Riesling. I love Rieslings, but it's a bad choice for a wedding. Go for a clean, crisp white and a soft, fruity, uncomplicated red.

Wine is expensive in Ireland and many couples are choosing to make the trip to France to stock up on good wine at a reasonable price. Do you have any advice for these people?

Paolo The same advice as above. If you're not sure of your own judgement, buying wine cheaply in a French hypermarket might result in a disastrous choice. It won't be expensive, but you might find your guests tipping their glasses into the pot plants. Only do this if you know what you're at and then you can save a fortune in excise duties.

Going abroad is not practical for everyone. For couples buying at home what would you recommend? (shops etc.)

Paolo A good start is John Wilson's book *100 Wines for Under €10*. If your budget runs to more than that check out the other books on wines on sale in Ireland. Don't re-invent the wheel, other people have tasted hundreds if not thousands of wines, so make use of that research. Occasionally Dunnes Stores do a 30% off deal on their wines, which make them really great value. If you're buying with a few months to go you can look out for bargains and special offers.

A recent trend in weddings is to use local organic produce and organic wines. Would you have any advice for couples sourcing organic wine in Ireland or abroad?

Paolo Organic grapes make organic wine. They don't guarantee good wine. There's a long process between the grapes and the final product of wine, so it's the skill of the wine-maker that counts. O'Brien's do a good range of organic wines called Novas from Chile which are also good wines.

Do you have anything to say about the champagne versus sparkling wine debate?

Paolo The bubbles in the bottle double the excise duty. It's about €2 on a bottle of wine and it's about €4 on a bottle of bubbly. And that's before our dear government adds the VAT at 21%, so you pay VAT on the cost of the wine, the transport and the duty — i.e. you pay 21% tax on the €4 tax. No wonder the stuff's expensive. A good sparkling wine is a perfect substitute for average champagne. Never forget, a lot of what you pay for champagne is for those huge advertising budgets, not for the wine in the bottle. Whatever the big brands would like you to believe, champagne is just a sparkling wine from that part of France called Champagne. No mystery, no magic ingredient. It's a sparkling wine. If you can find one that you like made somewhere else, it'll do just fine. Take your Tesco bubbly at €26.49. The government share of that is the 21% VAT included in the price — that's €5.57 — plus the €4 duty, or nearly a tenner. More than Tesco makes, more than the wholesaler makes, more than the producer makes.

Chapter Seven

The Cake

Non-virgins take note! Up until recent times, the cutting of the cake, once the sole responsibility of the bride, was symbolic of the bride's pending loss of virginity. Nowadays it is mainly another photo opportunity. Although sharing the cake around is symbolic of sharing the day with friends and family, you could argue that sharing a meal together covers things sufficiently and, like more and more people, decide to give it a miss. Or you could decide that it doesn't have to be a multi-storey affair that costs the price of a new television and so go with something less traditional. If it is a proper wedding cake you want, then remember to shop around, as prices can vary from bakery to bakery.

 First Decisions

No cake If it is not something you care either way about and you would rather redirect a wow in another direction, then just skip it. Most guests won't even notice.

Keep it simple Again if it is not your thing but you just want to have one for the sake of tradition, rather than being dwarfed by a five-tier sugar mountain, why not choose something simple or novelty, and pop some beautiful flowers on top. The display table can be enhanced if the bridal party set down their bouquets next to it.

Go high street A lot of the price of the cake is down to man hours getting the cake perfect, yet for much less you can get that ready-made perfect cake. Marks & Spencer sell very reasonably priced white wedding cakes. They taste delicious. It takes very little effort to dress the cakes with a nice cake topper and some flowers. The manager at my venue commented that they were her favourite cakes as they are 'so perfectly finished'. Marks & Spencer regularly have three layers for the price of two on offer and in total should cost around €75–€100. They sell cake tiers too but check if your venue has a stand already.

Copy artists Fallen in love with a cake? Take a photo of the cake along to another baker and get a cheaper price. Hometown bakers will often do just as good a job as a busy city baker.

☺ Self-sufficient

Self-bake If you enjoy baking and like a challenge, why not attend a cake-making class in the run-up to your wedding? Not only will you then be able to make your own cake, but with your new-found skills you can offer your services to friends and family for future weddings. (See *cakebox.ie*, *eveningclasses.ie*.)

Homemade As professional bakers operate on a business level, with staff and overheads, if you can source a home baker it should work out less. Check out the classified section of your local paper or the *Buy and Sell* to find people who make special cakes for extra income. Phone a cake decorating class and ask if the teacher would do your cake. Of course you might be lucky enough to have a cake maker in the family.

> **Clay toppers made to order, just like you**
> You can choose the theme, outfits, hairstyles and other details to make your figures unique to you. They are not cheap but they can jazz up a cake. This site is good for ideas too if you would like to try making your own cake topper using Fimo Clay. You might have enough time to practice.
> (See *claycorner.co.uk* and *polymerclaypit.co.uk*.)

Decorations Use fresh flowers, fruits and berries, and place the bridal bouquets around the base of the cake before the guests enter the dining room. You can also purchase cake decorations from Cakebox in Dun Laoghaire. (See *cakebox.ie*.)

Chocolate tier A novel idea is to purchase a cake stand on eBay and pack it full with individual chocolates, laid out on a bed of large white feathers. The effect is a dramatic tiered chocolate and feather display that will blow any cake out of the water.

> **The Edible Dress!**
> In 2006 Ukrainian baker Valentyn Shtefano had a surprise for his bride — he made her wedding dress out of flour, eggs, sugar and caramel. The edible dress — made of 1,500 cream puffs and weighing in at 20 lbs — took the 28-year-old baker two months to make, and by the end of the wedding reception, bride Viktoriya didn't want to take it off, much less devour it.

◀▷ Something Different

Cupcake mountain Novelty cakes in the form of a mountain of cupcakes are very popular for weddings. Each guest can have a cupcake. It looks amazing! For inspiration on how it can look, visit this London bakers: *crumbsanddoilies.co.uk*. As you will see on that site it can be great fun: there is a wedding featured in the blog section where a mountain of cupcakes is topped with a small white wedding cake. Perfect!

French fancies A wacky option is a tower of French fancies! If you don't take cakes too seriously this is the answer for you. Rows of French fancies lined together on a stand. You could make it even 'prettier' adding to it with feathers and putting a brightly coloured tablecloth under the display. Everyone loves French fancies. Especially good for a funky style wedding!

Chocolate wedding cake Have a big gooey chocolate wedding cake. Set it out on a table surrounded by chocolates. You don't need to tell the bakery it is for a wedding, and so you won't pay the wedding price. Delicious. If you are worried about not having enough to feed the crowd, order two large cakes; you will still save.

A sweet table or trolley rather than a single cake. A selection of cakes and pastries which guests can help themselves to. This will still work out cheaper than an elaborate wedding cake, and will probably have a much bigger wow factor. If you miss the wedding cake, have one white tier amidst the rest with your cake top and bridal design.

Croque en bouche Pyramid piled high with profiteroles. Guests help themselves to a ball or two each. Perfect for serving as dessert. (See *cakesonline.ie*.)

Cheesecake Everyone loves cheesecake. They look beautiful and can be covered in cream cheese icing for the white wedding look. Perfect for serving as dessert with fresh fruit or flowers on top.

The Cheese Wedding Cake Sheridans Cheesemongers can tailor-make a wedding cake for you, comprised of tiered stacks of cheese wheels, which when completed resembles the shape of a traditional wedding cake! Wily use of cake boards, pillars, empty cheese boxes and various other structural supports means Sheridans can go to great lengths to include your favourite cheeses on your tailor-made wedding cake. They will tailor-make this cake to suit your event and your pocket. This novel idea can be used as a cheese course or served with bread and chutney for a late evening snack for guests.

Cheese with a bloomy white rind looks white and fluffy like a traditional wedding cake. Cheese wheels of Gubbeen, Durrus, Tomme de Savoie, Knockanore Smoked, Lavistown, Ossau Iraty, Manchego, Clonmore, Cashel Blue and many more are all suitable for a cheese wedding cake, while most cheddars, Stilton and Shropshire Blue can all be cut into stackable layers.

Sheridans will decorate your cake to suit the theme or colour palette of your wedding. Seasonal fruits also add a great finishing touch to your cheese cake. Prices for cheese wedding cakes range from €80 to €350. However, Sheridans can tailor-make a cake to suit your price range and any other preferences. Sheridans have stores in Galway and Dublin. For more information see the cheese wedding cake at *www.sheridanscheesemongers.com.*

 ## Clever Tips

Avoid delivery and set-up costs by ordering your own cake and bringing it to the venue yourself.

Serve the cake as dessert Georgina Campbell's *Romantic Weddings* gives excellent run downs of the venues' policies on cake. You can see if the venue you like will allow cake to be served as dessert. Stretch it — using your cake as dessert is an excellent idea for cost saving, especially for a summer wedding. A light fresh cream sponge cake with strawberries is the nicest dessert you could have on a summer's day. Here is the perfect time for a large sponge cake in the kitchen and a small cake on display. You could also substitute a cake with a dessert table (see 'Something Different'). If you choose to serve your wedding cake as the sweet course the list is endless but choose a cake with all tiers the same. What are very suitable and easy to serve are chocolate cakes in all forms. Use all of it; saving a layer of cake for the christening is a cute idea but the storage involved and the possibility that it will taste horrible by then means you are better off just eating it!

> **If your venue doesn't have a cake stand** you can buy a variety of cake stands on eBay.

Enhance the size Go larger using Styrofoam. This is done surprisingly often. It is a great way to 'cut the cake' using a real layer between two identical fake layers. You can have a large sheet cake and a small cake can be used for display and the cake-cutting ceremony. The sheet cake, which is cheaper as it is just iced and requires no decoration, gets sliced and dished up in the kitchen.

Buying big – bargain big If you want to go the traditional route and buy a large decorated cake, don't just walk into a cake shop. Try instead to book your cake at a wedding fair where many cake stalls can fight for your business. This is much easier than trying to negotiate on the shop floor. You can play two cake stalls against one another and you never know.

🕐 Good Timing

Christmas What better time to get a good deal on a fruitcake iced snow white! If you are getting married at Christmas you are really going to make a saving. All the high street supermarkets will be selling large and small wedding cakes. Buy an assortment and next to the tree you have your cake.

Easter Getting married Easter week, this is the perfect time to substitute your cake with chocolate. A large bowl of chocolate eggs for each guest perhaps, in a large basket with blue gingham cloth. People love something different at weddings, something that sets your wedding apart.

🖱 Webguide

cakebox.ie In the cake photo gallery here you will find a four-tiered fun cake called 'Helter Skelter' for which you will pay €900. Prices are generally between €400 and €600. Cakebox also run wedding cake making courses. They also run day courses with intriguing titles like 'Chocolate Madness'.
cakesonline.ie If you are looking for the ideal dessert, a croque-en-boche is perfect. You will pay €170 for this.
claycorner.co.uk Cake toppers
crumbsanddoilies.co.uk Inspiration for cupcake mountains
eveningclasses.ie
polymerplaypit.co.uk Cake toppers
sheridanscheesemongers.com Cheese wedding cake
the-cake-gallery.com Kells, Co. Meath — For a three-tier iced wedding cake expect to pay €350 and upwards. Cake-maker Christina Quinn advises that for a less formal single-tier cake, such as a chocolate cake involving less work, you will pay approximately €100.

Chapter Eight

Entertainment

The entertainment is high on the list for a good wedding, alongside good food and wine. For you as a couple, this is the time in the evening when the mass is long over, everyone is fed and you have survived the speeches. There is a nice buzz of conversation while the tables are cleared and people are mingling and ordering drinks from the bar. You are probably tired with chatting, it's time to kick off those heels, loosen the tie and enjoy a good dance and a drink or two!

※ First Decisions

Band and DJ Typically an Irish wedding involves a band and a DJ. A wedding band can cost up to €2,000, sometimes more, to play for two and a half hours.

DJ solo More recently couples are choosing to have a DJ take care of the entire evening. Live bands, although a fun and interactive element to a wedding, are not for everyone. Anyone who has been to a few Irish weddings knows that often the band can be excessively loud, play very dated and old-fashioned music and charge a lot for this service. With a DJ you have control over the music and entertainment, and you pay less too. If you think a band is necessary for 'the older people', then remember that your DJ can mix music from the 1920s through to the 2000s, keeping all your guests happy. And at a fraction of the price of a five-piece band.

☺ Self-sufficient

iPod According to the *Chicago Tribune* (13 July 2006), iPods are now all the rage for weddings in the States.

> Music is very important to us both, so we had a music playlist made on iTunes.com for our iPod. All you need for the vast majority of sound/PA systems is a mini jack to phono cable and you're in business. Take great care in constructing your playlist, after all it is mainly for background music and remember the musical generation gap of the guests.
>
> **Ruth and Ultan, Sligo**

Two for the price of one and a half Although music at a drinks reception is really not required, it can be done more economically. If you have a musician playing in the church, why not ask this musician to come along to the reception to play as your guests arrive at the hotel. One more hour from a musician already booked will be much cheaper than a new person.

Advertisement Put an advertisement up in a local music school. Many student musicians are too busy with their college work to actively seek out nixers. If you go to them and offer a reasonable price for a couple of hours' music, you will definitely save on the services advertised in the directory or online.

CD During the meal you can ask your hotel to play music of your choice over the sound system. Most function rooms will have this facility.

 **Clever Tips**

First dance If you are doing the traditional first dance and dance with your father etc. don't assume everyone knows the drill (like I did). In advance of the day tell everyone that they should be near the dance floor when the band or DJ are getting started. You don't want it to turn into a frantic rush to find the bridesmaid or best man while you are enjoying your first dance.

Don't judge your wedding by the dance floor A packed dance floor is great. It is an obvious sign of great fun being had by many. Depending on how long the day has been, what sort of guests you have, where the dance floor is in relation to the bar, don't fall into a panic if your dance floor is empty. This does not mean people are not enjoying themselves. People will want to socialise as well as dance. It may take a while for the evening to warm up or maybe people prefer to chill out and chat. Personally, I prefer to socialise at weddings and keep the dancing to a minimum!

Lobby talk For many reasons guests will inevitably prefer to sit in the lobby or in an adjacent bar away from the music. This is their preference and you should not be offended by it; dancing and music are not for everyone, usually for the reason below.

Sound Many people complain about the sound levels of a band or DJ, be it at a twenty-first birthday or a wedding. It is quite irritating to spend the evening competing with speakers you would normally find at a rock concert. I will never understand why bands do this.

Guests' rooms Try and ensure that elderly guests and those with babies and small children are not in rooms above the function room. There is nothing worse than trying to sleep to the sound of a party below. Hotels tend to give these rooms to wedding guests assuming they will be at the wedding until the end.

◖D Something Different

Short live act You could arrange for a small céilí, piano player or instrumental group in the lobby while the room is being cleared or for the beginning of the evening. A group playing instruments will only require a few stools. You will have a bit of live music before the DJ at a fraction of the cost of a band.

Anything else? Depending on what type of wedding you are having, there really is no limit to what you can do: a magician for a wedding with lots of children, fireworks for a Halloween wedding (about €500 - €1,000 for fifteen minutes), Irish dancers for an Irish/American wedding.

Compliments of the bride Some couples are deciding to add a little fun to boring old toilet cubicles, putting framed poems, balloons, jokes and a basket of 'emergency supplies' such as tights, matches, mints, plasters. If not already supplied it is nice to include hand wash and hand cream too.

 # Eco-Ethical Eye

Whether it is unethical to subject your guests to too much 'Red Rose Café' at this point is up to you; everyone's tastes are different. However, try to get a good mix of music and if you can have a look over the playlist in advance, you might want to request some of your favourite songs.

WARNING

If you are going with a relative or friend, be it band or DJ, make sure that the relative or friend has performed before. Your wedding is not the occasion for them to try out their new act.

 # Webguide

irishweddingdj.com An example of one of the many professional wedding DJ services available in Ireland
iTunes.com To compile an iPod playlist

Ruairi Finnegan on Hiring a DJ

Ruairi Finnegan of *irishweddingdj.com* talks about hiring a DJ for your wedding and the savings that can be made at no cost to your entertainment.

With an ever-changing wedding culture many couples are opting for a DJ-led evening rather than the traditional band. A professional disc jockey can provide you with all the ingredients to make your night very fun and memorable at a fraction of the cost of a full band.

A DJ will have advantage over a band in that he can change the music to suit the dance floor rather than being confined to a playlist, allowing more creativity and spontaneity. Music recorded by the original artist is authentic and a DJ can play up to 150 songs on the night, whereas your average band's playlist is just a fraction of that.

On a practical level DJs take very little time to set up if the speeches run over, and they can regulate the sound if need be while maintaining a great atmosphere.

Booking the cheapest option is often the most tempting when booking a DJ. Resist this temptation. For that bit extra to hire an experienced *wedding* DJ you have someone on board who knows how to carry out all the wedding traditions and work with the kind of diverse audience you'll find at a wedding — someone capable of not just playing music, but motivating your guests. He needs to read the crowd, getting them dancing and keeping them there for the rest of the night. Experience at a twenty-first or a club will not guarantee the DJ knows the music that will get your older relatives on the dance floor!

Make sure that you ask for references and make sure the DJ you meet is the DJ who carries out your wedding. I would also strongly advise couples to make sure you discuss the music with the disc jockey prior to the night.

All of our disc jockeys are dressed formally for all events, something which I feel is important at a wedding. They are also friendly to guests and carry a vast music collection to try to ensure all of your special requests are entertained.

But the most important thing is to relax and enjoy yourself.

Expect to pay €300 upwards for a DJ. For a full evening it can cost anything from €500. This is inclusive of sound and lighting equipment. Further expenses such as travel should be agreed at time of booking.

Looking Good

Chapter Nine

The Dress

Feeling good and looking good on your wedding day are more important than any amount of flowers, fancy cars or a five-star hotel. Okay, all those things *and* looking good would be a home run, but feeling confident in yourself and looking fantastic on your day is a very good start. Be sure to allocate enough money towards your dress and a little more for splashing out on some luxury. Getting contact lenses or having your hair coloured in a good salon might make a big difference to confidence on the day, so it is money well spent. Of course it goes without saying, but I'll say it all the same: paying attention to diet and exercise in the lead-up to the day costs nothing and will do more for your mood and your figure than anything you can buy in the shops.

✸ First Decisions

What to pay? Many Irish brides are paying up to €3,000 on the dress. (Let's not even mention Vera Wang.) The average is between €800 and €2,000. If there is one thing the wedding industry adores it is that wide-eyed bride looking in the shop window. The mark-up on these dresses is astounding; there is no defending the price. But while the market continues to pay, the prices will continue to rise. For those of you who are not happy to pay these extortionate prices, follow me!

Where to look?

Go online, go online, go online! Online bridal stores stock most designer names at a fraction of the price you will pay in a bridal shop. This is an excellent money-saving opportunity. Visit the message boards on the wedding sites, where a quick search will throw up hundreds of satisfied brides, like me, who bought online. Reputable online shops, who are authorised dealers of the designers, will provide you with the exact dress you want. There are clear returns policies on the dresses and 50 percent payment on delivery options in some of the stores. The safest way to go about buying online is to speak to other brides and get recommendations. Then email the various online stores with the details of the dress you like. For example, visit *hillcrestbridal.co.uk* to see what you can get online. Purchasing from a UK online store is preferable to US sites as you are not liable for customs duty. However, there may be a wider range available in the US and it will still work out cheaper than a bridal shop.

> Afraid of purchasing over the net? Read the tips from internet expert Alex French in Shopping Tips, on page 15.

Can't find it online? If you do fall in love with a dress, you can't always be sure it will be online. If not, now that you have pinned down a style you know suits you, you might decide to be brave and order a *similar* dress online. Any reputable website will have a detailed returns policy, so if you are unhappy with the dress the transaction will have only cost you in postage.

If you don't want to go down that route, make sure before you purchase to do a thorough search for the dress in other bridal shops across the country; so many brides are disappointed after their purchase to discover their dress bought in Dublin was €300 cheaper in Donegal. Visit the high street shops that are selling beautiful dresses at a third of the prices of those in the bridal shops. But before you buy anything, make sure you have visited the discount sales and tried on similar styles. (See *bridalsales.ie*.)

> Is it cheaper up North? Get the price and do the conversion on xe.com.

> When purchasing online check the measurements chart. Too much altering might damage the dress. You can easily alter a dress to make it smaller but to do the reverse is a major job.

The high street As discussed in Chapter One, the high street has finally realised that the bridal market is there to be cracked. And so we see beautiful dresses being sold at a fraction of the price you will pay for 'designer' bridal wear. Why? Details like machine sewing rather than tailored finishing or machine work rather than hand beading. Hands up anyone who can tell the difference? They might use man-made materials which are less expensive than natural fibres. Again, if it looks good for the day, does it matter? Debenhams and Monsoon are the current leaders in Ireland, with a wonderful selection of dresses to choose from.

Don't want that bridal look? Then steer clear of bridal shops altogether. Many modern brides are not interested in the white corset with full skirt or anything like it. Consider boutique shops or department stores for evening dresses and ball gowns. For example, Costume in Dublin is a high-end clothing boutique which sources evening dresses specifically for brides who are looking for something more toned down, not obviously bridal but still glamorous for the day. Karen Millen also has dresses suitable for more relaxed weddings. At the same time, you will find many different types of bridesmaids' dresses in bridal stores, some of which are perfect for the bride herself.

I saw my dress in a bridal shop and before paying a deposit I decided to email some online bridal stores (see Webguide). Within 24 hours I had a chirpy reply from *netbride.com* telling me they had the dress I liked for €499 including postage and packing. This same dress was hanging on a rail in Dublin with a price tag of €1,600. Of course when I mentioned this to family and friends, all agreed there *had* to be a catch. *You should stick to what you know. You'll be stung* with customs tax. There was no catch, the dress was perfect, I wasn't taxed for some reason but if I had been I would have still saved over €1,000 on my dress!

A second outing

Consider how many lonely, dusty wedding dresses lie in attics, long forgotten. A recent trend is to let the dress have another day out. 'Ugh', I hear you say, 'second-hand!' Correction — not second-hand, simply *once-worn*. Before giving them to the shop, newlywed brides will have paid a hefty price for them to be dry cleaned back into their pre-wedding state. No matter how beautiful and brand new they still look, like cars, wedding dresses lose much of their value once they have been owned by someone else. Cash in!

I came across a message from a newlywed bride on *weddingsonline.ie* advertising two bridesmaids' dresses. As it turned out when I phoned she only lived two miles away from me. She called to the house with the dresses and they were an instant success. On her wedding day at a cost of €950, she had these two beautiful Watters and Watters designer dresses with fantastic cream wraps. At my wedding, just over six months later, at a cost of €250, I had my two bridesmaids in the same dresses! I couldn't believe my luck, she had even put the tags back on!

If you are purchasing a dress from another bride, on eBay or on a wedding website, *without* trying it on, remember internet browsers render colours in different ways, so what you see in a photograph might not be what you get. Try to get a good idea of the condition of the garment, and the exact sizing, before you commit. If at all possible, try the dress on or request a good photograph before purchasing.

Charity meets bridal When people hear charity shops they think musty, overpacked rails. Recently opened on George's Street, Dublin, Oxfam Occasions is far from musty! It has over a hundred never-worn and end-of-season gowns donated from stores like Alfred Angelo, Forever Yours and Virgin Brides as well as those donated by the public. The room upstairs in Oxfam is well decorated with fitting rooms, long mirrors and a couch for your mother or sister to sit back and watch the show! Gowns start at €100 to €350 and they also have bridesmaids'/flower girl dresses, veils, tiaras and shoes. They rotate the dresses every six months, so try to visit the shop the day of their next rotation for the latest dresses! Barnardos in Dun Laoghaire, Co. Dublin, also offer a similar service selling new and once-worn dresses.

Once-worn shops An example of a shop that will purchase your dress from you is Encore Bridal in Clondalkin, Dublin. Encore offers brides a large selection of once-worn designer wedding and bridesmaids' dresses. This shop may have the dress you are looking for at a much lower price than the bridal shops. Or you could sell your dress to Encore after the wedding.

> **Home Store**
> An online store selling wedding dresses at a discount rate is *dreambridal.ie*. This is a network of women selling dresses from home. You can try the dresses on in their houses. Available in Galway, Clare and Meath.

Rent Consider renting a gown instead of purchasing. These dresses are only rented out if they look new and that is all you want. You will still pay €500 or so for the dress. An example of a shop renting dresses is High Society in Greystones, Co. Wicklow, and Fairytale Brides in Delvin, Co. Westmeath.

☺ Self-sufficient

Be inventive If you are browsing boutiques or department stores and you spot a beautiful white dress that flatters your figure but you feel it doesn't seem quite special enough, you could consider a simple alteration: some beading, a lace overcoat, some feathers, removing the straps, adding a fur stole or accessorising the look. Small changes can significantly alter the look of the dress while still maintaining the flattering shape.

Have it made Another way to save money on your gown is to have someone make your dress. This is a high-risk venture and you will need to be sure you trust your dressmaker, as there is no turning back once the dress is made. And there is a lot of work involved in making a wedding dress so it will still be expensive. But it may save you a couple of hundred euro. The best thing to do first though is to try on as many styles as you can because what you think will look good may not. You can then narrow down the styles that suit you and choose a photograph of a dress rather than dreaming up a dress, which could be risky.

Look for recommendations on wedding sites. You could also locate a seamstress by investigating whether any that work doing alterations for bridal shops are 'moonlighting' on the side. If you are really daring, you can approach a fashion school and have a student design and make your gown as a project. Make sure it is a graduate or near-graduate with a portfolio to prove they can deliver the goods. *Always* chat to someone else who had their dress made by the designer, and see their previous work. Never put your wedding dress in the hands of an amateur you know little or nothing about.

> **Gift of a dress**
> Rather than getting a washing machine or stereo system, mention to your parents early on that you would love help buying the dress.

🕐 Good Timing

Plan in advance Most shops need to pre-order the dresses four to six months in advance.

Discontinued gowns will be cheaper but will also require a little effort to locate. Sample or display gowns are even cheaper. Many brides queue outside these sales in anticipation so they are worth the effort of locating and travelling to them. Keep an eye on the web for sales on *bridalsales.net*.

Borrow a friend's or relative's gown. If you fall in love with someone's dress — perhaps a workmate's or a friend from another circle to your own

— be brave and ask for a lend of it. This would be particularly recommended if you normally find it difficult to get clothes to fit well — if you see a friend in a dress you know would suit you, don't be afraid to ask.

☼ Clever Tips

Be a valued customer There is usually no repeat custom in bridal shops and so you are less likely to get any free extras unless you haggle *before* deciding. Ask for free services such as alterations, or get a tiara thrown in or a generous discount. If they won't agree, go elsewhere, simple as that.

Stay open Remember to be open to ideas. I was convinced I wanted a lace dress. I had pictured myself in my mind's eye in lace. When I tried it on in the shop it couldn't have looked worse! A dress that looks perfect in a picture in a magazine might not suit you. Look at a wide variety of styles. Try them on. You'll soon know what style suits you best.

- Get your dress altered while wearing the exact shoes you plan to wear on the day.
- Have your dress fitting the day of your hair trial. See hairdresser Anthony Murray's advice on page 97.

Accessorise You can make the simplest dress look completely different through the use of a fur stole or dramatic jewellery.

Networking – Pair Up or Sell On

Pair up It is also an option to pair up with a bride online by checking if anyone is interested in your dress. You could leave a message on a board, for example: <<B2B July 2008 would like to purchase Size 12, Mon Cheri *Lucy*, perfect for the taller bride. Let me know if anyone is interested in purchasing together.>> If this dress costs €1,400 and you find a bride getting married soon who is interested in sharing the cost of the dress and re-selling it afterwards, you will save a considerable amount.

Sell on You may not be able to compromise on a dress that you have fallen in love with, but you could, sensibly, plan to re-sell it. If you take a little extra care on the day and line up immediate dry cleaning afterwards, you could have it sold in a matter of weeks. However, do not leave it too late as your dress will be considered out of date quite quickly.

> To buy or sell, or simply collect, visit *weddingsonline.ie/discussion, buyandsell.ie, jumbletown.ie.*

> Shipments sent from outside the EU may be liable for customs duty, excise duty and VAT. This will add to the price, although it will not detract from the major saving you are making. US bridal companies have been criticised for marking down the value of packages in order to assist customers in avoiding these duties. Be aware that knowingly avoiding duties leaves you open to prosecution. For more on this see *houseofbrides.com.*

Eco-Ethical Eye

If you prefer to purchase your own organic materials to have the dress made, visit *organicsilks.co.uk.* Of course the most environmentally conscious thing to do is to purchase a dress from another bride and give it another day out!

Live on Rather than let your wedding dress sit in a wardrobe growing more out of fashion by the month and yellowed by the day, let it live again. Drop your dress into Oxfam or Barnardos and know that they can earn valuable cash to pass on to those in need.

Chapter Ten

The Bridal Party — Seven Savings

1. For bridesmaids and flower girls all the same tips apply from 'The Dress'. **Buying online** is even more popular for these dresses than for wedding dresses. Have a look at *rkbridal.com*, which is a very popular site for sourcing bridesmaids' dresses. Borrowing or buying dresses from another bride, like I did, is also popular as, let's face it, bridesmaids' dresses rarely suit other occasions.

2. **Saving by elimination** A ready-made saving here is if you just have one bridesmaid. One bridesmaid means a knock-on saving of only one best man. You are adding at least €200 to your bill for each bridesmaid you have. There are so many other, less expensive ways of involving

friends and family. If you have to choose, why not all go out for dinner together and pick a name from a hat. That's fair.

3. **High street** Now that the high street has twigged how big the wedding market is, lucky you can really benefit from this. You can make brilliant savings in the form of beautiful bridesmaids' dresses, and stores such as Debenhams sell and rent men's dress suits. For further details see general tips on shopping at the start of the book.

4. **Second-hand** There is no harm repeating myself here. As I said in Chapter Nine, I bought my bridesmaids' dresses from a newlywed and got €950 worth of dresses for €250! My bridesmaids had the opportunity to try the dresses on and decide, and we had fun doing the shopping for shoes and accessories to match, so we didn't miss out on a girlie afternoon.

5. **Go your own way** Many brides decide they don't want the hassle of trying to co-ordinate two or three dresses on different figures and tastes. Instead they give their bridesmaids a colour and a budget and send them shopping. That way, each woman can choose a dress they feel comfortable in while still looking the part.

6. **Black dresses for bridesmaids** There are so many beautiful black dresses out there, you are bound to find a suitable black dress in a non-bridal shop, for usually a quarter of the price of the designer dresses.

7. **Little ones, big bills** A page boy outfit to rent can cost over €100. A dress for a flower girl along with a shrug or shawl will cost too. Children wear beautiful outfits to weddings these days and will look a picture in the photos anyway. If you have a few younger girls at the wedding, why not avoid singling out one and make them all feel special? Ask their parents to dress them in white dresses and you can arrange sashes/hair bows that match the bridesmaids. This is a cheap and effective way of involving everyone, and it will look beautiful in the photographs. For little boys you could arrange dickie bows in the colour of the bridesmaids and send them to their parents in advance of the day. See *lantz.ie/accessories/*. For children's bow ties try eBay.

Groomsmen Make sure to get a 'groom goes free' offer on your suits. Men's suit hire companies are tripping over each other for your business at bridal fairs. So, be sure to get the same offer even if you have just walked in off the street. When the final bill is added up, ask for a further discount and then ask it to be rounded down! If you don't ask you won't get. Be brave . . . think of what you can spend the savings on.

Keep it modern The waistcoat, cravat and tails look is not for everyone. I would say at every second wedding I have attended or heard about in the last two years the groom has worn a straightforward suit and tie. Well put together buttonholes dress up the simplest of outfits. The advantage of doing this is that the suit can be worn on many more occasions. If it is a regular coloured suit your groomsmen may have the perfect attire already. If not, it will be very easy to rent similar suits and ties to create the perfect bridal party.

Blacktie, White Tie If you don't want the waistcoat cravat look but would rather a more formal look than a standard suit, the groomsmen can go black tie, or wear the very sophisticated white tie look too.

Debenhams hire out menswear at reasonable rates.

Page Boy If it is a summer's day a little waistcoat and matching bow tie is all that is needed. It can cost up to €120 to rent a full page boy outfit. So buy the basics in Dunnes Stores and source the rest online.

Chapter Eleven

Accessories — Nine Ways to Save Money

Costume jewellery, necklaces, bracelets, handbags, hair clips, fur stoles . . . They may be considered 'little extras' but extras are one of the things that can tip a budget over the limit. When it comes to accessories you really can halve the bill. A handmade, Irish-designed, jewel-encrusted tiara would look fantastic I am sure, but you'd be surprised how fantastic something very similar on eBay for a tenth of the price will look too! First rule here: stay out of the bridal shops for accessories.

1. **Beg or borrow** Some of your friends or family will probably have been married in recent years. You can be sure they have once-worn cufflinks, strings of pearls and tiaras in their wardrobes. In particular ask to borrow a veil because veils do not last, they normally discolour and rot in wardrobe conditions. Be brave and ask friends and family before hitting the shops. I didn't wear a veil or the traditional tiara but I was offered so many I found the offers hard to refuse! It is also madness how many ring cushions are sitting in the tops of wardrobes all dressed up with nowhere to go. My ring cushion has done four weddings now in two years. Couples really do love to see the items they spent money on getting another day out!

2. **Do not buy jewellery in a bridal shop** If you want to save money you can find something just as nice in a department store or online. Marks & Spencer has jewellery specifically designed for weddings but not priced for weddings, from pearl chokers to delicate silver crosses. Shops like Claire's Accessories are perfect for items that only need to last a day.

3. **Costume** At this expensive time it is not wise to splash out on jewellery to last a lifetime. Maybe your first anniversary is a more appropriate time for real pearl earrings or a new watch. In the meantime consider this: can you tell real pearl from a fake? Can you tell diamond from glass? If you can, you are in a minority. Search out some nice expensive-looking costume jewellery, it won't be hard.

4. **Little boutiques** There are so many little Aladdin's caves full of the most beautiful designs. For example, Costello and Costello in Dublin sell a beautiful selection of jewellery in all colours and styles with matching handbags and wraps. Prices range from €9 to €150 — you'll be surprised though at what you can get for so little.

5. **Hat** For more casual weddings a hat makes a carefree and lighthearted alternative to a bridal veil and a formal bridal bouquet. There are also those beautiful Italian style lace capes.

6. **Hair** For hair accessories go no further than your nearest department store or Accessorize shop.

7. **Make it** It is a very simple process to attach a veil to a headpiece, so why not arrange your own? You can buy the supplies for around €30 in Hickeys Fabric Stores and arrange for your dressmaker to put it together. This is a massive saving compared to the €200-plus price tags on cathedral-length veils in bridal shops.

> If you feel like learning a new skill why not make your own jewellery? See *eveningcourses.ie* or *ncad.ie*.

8. **Bead shops** I bought pearls and small crystals from a bead shop along with a little bag of wires for twisting into my hair and my bridesmaids' hair. I added just the right amount of sparkle to our hair. Your nearest bead shop will provide you with some Swarovski crystals, and attaching them to a hairpin or wire is easier than finger painting. The effect is beautiful and will cost you less than €5. So if you want to make, or commission, your own tiara or jewellery hairclips for the day, you should visit a bead shop where you can purchase the beads, and the owner can direct you to a jewellery maker.

9. **Online** There are excellent resources online for purchasing accessories. Any good web shop will have a returns policy, so if the necklace doesn't suit the dress, you can send it back. **Fake it** — you can purchase a fake fur stole online for €50, compared to over €200 for a similar item in bridal shops! See *faux.uk.com*.

Chapter Twelve

Ten Things about Rings

As your engagement and wedding rings are something you will probably wear throughout your life, make sure you are not ripped off. Wherever you buy your rings, make sure the company is reputable. I am going to assume that for many of you who are reading this book, an engagement ring is already on your finger. If not, and you have decided on a diamond, you can find excellent information online. Whatever you do, don't assume the person in the jewellery shop knows what they are talking about. Shop around.

1. Go for what you *like* the look of. I am sure a jeweller will recommend that you consider the value of the metal, the properties, etc., but all

you need to check is that it won't be high maintenance in terms of polishing and that it is good quality. After that, you should simply pick a ring you like the look of.

2. **Buy online** For discount prices visit *diamond.ie* and *diamondsandgoldireland.com*. Why? As reviewed in the *Irish Independent*, 'like Dell and Ryanair, this jewellery company cut out the middleman'. *e-weddingbands.com* sells amazing value jewellery, recommended by Irish brides on message boards. It is a US site but mails to Ireland via FedEx for $48 and you will incur customs duty but you will still pay a lot less for your bands. Platinum wedding rings from *e-weddingbands.com* cost €200. All you need to do is figure out the style you like and your finger measurement — it is that simple. All four websites confirm they do not sell conflict diamonds (see next page).

3. **Plain gold bands** are much cheaper than ornamental ones with gems, and you are also very unlikely to find yourself bored with the style five years down the road.

4. **Getting a wedding ring made** will cost more than buying it off the shelf.

5. **Groom, have you thought about titanium?** Platinum is expensive because it is a precious metal; however, the similar but stronger metal titanium is becoming a popular choice lately. It is an abundant metal and so it is a lot less expensive than platinum. It is actually used in body implant surgery as few people have a reaction to it. Platinum is considered of 'higher value' as a precious metal; however, this is only relevant if you are planning on re-selling. Jewellery is not an investment.

6. What about **silver** instead of gold?

7. **'His/Her'** packages can save money.

8. For your engagement ring, **purchase stones and setting separately** and then have the stones placed into the setting.

9. Check out **antique shops** and sales. You never know what you will find there.

10. If you find a diamond you like, there is the possibility of having the stone **reset** into a different wedding band. Or even a diamond necklace with many diamonds can be used to create a diamond-encrusted band. Similarly if you have family jewellery that is never worn you should really consider modernising it. You may already have the stones to make a fantastic wedding ring!

> Looking for a thin gold band to complement my antique wedding ring, I was told in two shops that I would find it very difficult to find and would probably need to have it made (€250). Ten minutes later in an antiques shop I found the perfect ring for €115!

Eco-Ethical Eye

The website *nodirtygold.org* is about sourcing responsible stones and metals. Or you might consider a second-hand or antique ring rather than impacting further on the environment by purchasing a newly manufactured one.

Conflict diamonds

"Diamonds are forever", it is often said. But lives are not. We must spare people the ordeal of war, mutilations and death for the sake of conflict diamonds.'
Martin Chungong Ayafor,
Chairman of the Sierra Leone Panel of Experts

Conflict diamonds are diamonds that originate from areas controlled by forces or factions opposed to legitimate and internationally recognised governments, and are used to fund military action in opposition to those governments, or in contravention of the decisions of the UN Security Council.

For an example of ethical policies, visit *diamondandgoldireland.com* and *diamond.ie*. Appleby Jewellers have even produced a brochure about their ethical practices. There is a quotation from the *diamond.ie* website: '*Whilst diamonds are, for the most part, bought and worn for love, they are used in parts of Africa to fund war. Diamond.ie complies with the United Nations resolution for peace. We totally abhor the sale of conflict diamonds.'*

Ask your jeweller where the diamonds they sell originated and whether or not they are certified, and be sure they are not conflict diamonds.

Fairtrade Check out Silver Chilli (*silverchilli.com*) for beautiful fairtrade jewellery.

Eco Have you considered a wooden wedding ring? See *touchwoodrings.com*. These rings are sustainable, and perfect for anyone allergic to metals too. The designs are surprisingly beautiful.

Chapter Thirteen

Shoes

'Bridal' shoes are sold in bridal shops and specialist shoe shops. Prices can start at around €100 and upwards. They are the satin kind that you will never wear again, as they look so much like *wedding shoes*. This is another mystery, why white or ivory satin shoes soar in price when the word 'bridal' is placed before them. Obviously it is important that the shoes you wear on your wedding day are comfortable, but they don't need to last. They don't need to be Italian designed, hand-finished Jimmy Choos; in fact they don't even need to look *that* fantastic as they are usually hidden under layers of dress. So here is yet another area where it is best to source your purchase outside the bridal world. Thankfully in this country there are enough debutant balls, graduation balls and gala events to ensure that formal shoes are stocked in ordinary shops. Simple white sandals are not hard to find on the high street. If you have a straightforward foot you can even go online.

My bridesmaids wore cream shoes that were €27 each in the Marks & Spencer sale (down from €60). My shoes, €30, were dainty white sandals in the end of summer sale. For a June wedding, wearing a full skirt, I could not justify spending over €100 on a shoe that would only peep out from under my skirt from time to time. I spent the change on a foot massage and pedicure!

✸ First Decisions

High street Shoe shops and department stores such as Next have rows and rows of every kind of shoe. You can guarantee if you keep an eye out in the months before your wedding, you will chance upon a suitable pair of white sandals or shoes for less than €50. Many stock 'bridal' shoes at a fraction of the price too. Clarke's, Marks & Spencer, Shoe Rack in Dublin, to name a few, all stock white and ivory shoes.

Borrowing Don't be afraid to ask another bride. Anyone who paid a high price for bridal shoes will be relieved to see them have another day out. Chances are they are sitting in the box since she slipped them off the night of her wedding! The same advice goes for the groom; if your brother has dress shoes that will fit you, borrow them.

Shoes online If the message boards are anything to go by, this is a very popular choice for brides these days. If you are one of the lucky ones with straightforward feet, try *bridalshoes.co.uk* or *eBay.ie*. All good sites have a returns policy which will be very helpful, but you will have to post them back, which with shoes will be expensive.

Black shoes Many bridesmaids' dresses are suited to simple black shoes so if you can get away with it at all you should. They are a safe bet and shoes that the girls can wear again so you need not worry about paying for them. Just let them off with a couple of pointers and things should work out fine.

☺ Self-sufficient

Shoe dying kits for bridesmaids. For some reason the dresses we choose for bridesmaids are rarely average colours and so it can be impossible pairing up. If you find the perfect shoe in a light colour, it might be worth dying them to match. For the bride, many designer bridal shoes are sold specifying they are suitable for dying. So if you want to splash out you may have the option of turning them into shoes you can wear again.

Clip-ons Purchase plain shoes from a shoe store and decorate with clip-ons. You can buy shoe clips on eBay and glue on a beautiful brooch — a simple and effective way to turn plain shoes into bridal shoes.

🕐 Good Timing

Sales, sales, sales! Wait till the end of summer sales to buy your shoes. There are racks and racks of shoes to choose from.

◐ Something Different

Getting married abroad? Pack some white flip-flops. If it is a sweltering day it will be a welcome relief after the ceremony.

Colour If there is any detailing on your dress in another colour, you should seriously consider getting shoes to match. One poster on a wedding message board laughed that her shoes were €35 because they are gold, like the embroidery across her skirt. The exact same style shoes in white were priced at €150! It really looks great too.

Annie Gribbon on Make-up

Annie is the founder of the Face2 Make-Up range at Make-Up Forever on Clarendon Street, Dublin (*face2.ie*). Annie regularly features on Off the Rails and Ireland AM playing a vital role in communicating the new trends and international advances in cosmetics to the Irish public. Her career has brought her around the world, working with numerous celebrities including U2, Alicia Silverstone, the Corrs, Pierce Brosnan, Debbie Harry and Kate Hudson, to name but a few! Here Annie shares some secrets about bridal make-up.

This day, more than any other day in your life, you will want to look good and feel good. Your husband, your guests, and your photographer — everyone will be focusing on you. It is essential that you feel confident and happy.

I wouldn't be in this business if I didn't believe, passionately, that make-up is one of the most important things for a bride to get right on the day. What is the point of putting all this effort into finding the perfect dress if your make-up is done badly? A professional make-up artist will apply make-up that will suit your skin tone and your eyes, enhance your features and, most importantly, keep you beautiful all day long.

No expensive dress or make-up can disguise a tired, worn-out face and dull hair. Looking good and feeling good starts with what you put *into* your body — eating and sleeping well in the lead-up to the day, drinking lots of water, exfoliating your skin before a shower, hair removal, shaping your eyebrows, maintaining good nails. None of these things will leave you out of pocket: a simple bottle of nail strengthener, a loofah, some home treatments that cost very little; they will make all the difference on the day. If this is not already part of your routine, start now — making this effort is important not just for your wedding day but for your marriage too!

Brides don't tend to prioritise themselves. This is an Irish habit, spending thousands on food and wine for your guests, on cake and decorations and not allocating some money on the day, and in the lead-up to the day, towards feeling and looking good. If you don't feel a professional will make a difference, at least have a trial or a lesson. You will find a well-trained make-up artist can make you look as natural as you want.

In photography, especially digital, everything shows up. Make-up should be blended well and any facial hair taken care of prior to the day. Correct make-up will also ensure that you are not bleached out by the flash; it is very important to wear the correct colour for your skin tone.

With the stress levels high on the morning of your wedding, it is quite settling to take time out, have your hair styled and make-up applied. And if your bridesmaids have their make-up done professionally, then everyone will complement each other perfectly.

When you are under stress many hormonal and neurological reactions within your body can cause redness, blotchy skin, a shiny face from extra perspiration. A professional can correct this using green or yellow base, which balances out the colour. If you are doing your own make-up and you are prone to redness, you should purchase a suitable product in advance. Have powder at the ready on the day to touch up your face.

Sip water the morning of the wedding. Keep sipping. It is good if you are stressed or nervous, keeping you cool and calm. Alcohol is not recommended.

Chat to your bridesmaids about what they plan to wear on the day. Badly applied make-up, dramatic eye shadow — these are things that can show up much worse in photographs than they already do in reality, knocking the overall look off balance.

Every woman, getting married or not, should have a make-up lesson. This is an investment! There are so many tricks — enhancing your eyes, blending, using powder to minimise shine. All these skills will ensure your make-up will survive all those kisses outside the church. If you are doing your own make-up please go for a good professional lesson and buy good products.

I will never understand the obsession with fake tan, it is an addiction! In Victorian times the bride's pale skin against the white was considered beautiful. Well cared for pale skin is beautiful and youthful looking. It is certainly more beautiful than streaky skin or a bride that turns dark brown just for the day of her wedding! Tan also enhances wrinkles and can make you look tired and years older than you are. No amount of professional make-up can undo some of the disasters caused by fake tan. Is it really worth the risk? If you want a little colour, a few sessions on the sunbed will do the trick, remembering to cover your face of course.

Have a trial before booking. It is important that you are happy with the person you choose on the day. You could have the trial the day of your hen. Don't assume that your local beauty therapist is skilled as a make-up artist. A make-up artist that is used to doing brides on a regular basis is best. Also, test products in advance of the day; you don't want to have your first facial the week of the wedding or have a severe reaction to the glue in fake lashes.

I can only recommend our range of make-up (Face2 in Make-up Forever) because we have everything a bride could want and they are good value too compared with many other well-known brands. Our products are used professionally in fashion, on television, in advertising, even on babies for photo shoots, so it is essential that they suit all skin types, they are well tested, they stay on and they don't dry out like a lot of products do.

Here are some tips:
- Use a lightweight moisturiser under foundation that is absorbed readily into the skin to ensure even coverage.
- Select the perfect shade by blending a small amount onto the side of the face. The correct colour should 'disappear' into your skin and match with the neck colour.
- Apply liquid make-up with fingertips and use a damp sponge to blend; only apply concealer if necessary.
- Check your make-up in good daylight to ensure the foundation is properly blended and there is no tideline between the face and neck.

- Apply loose powder over your foundation with a velour powder puff, removing any excess with a powder brush. Powder is the key to keeping foundation in place, especially on the day of your wedding when you will perspire more. You don't want a shiny face in the photographs.
- Invest in a good set of brushes. Using the right tools makes it easier to apply make-up like experts. Brushes and applicators contained in the products you buy are too small and of poor quality if you are trying to create a polished appearance. Remember, always wash your brushes regularly with mild shampoo or specialised brush cleaner to keep them in good condition.
- Use matte eye shadows for a natural look. Never use a dark shadow on the entire lid as it closes the eye. Instead use a base colour and gradually apply deeper tone into the socket getting lighter towards the brow bone.
- Eyeliner is a wonderful way to define the lash line and accentuate the eyes.
- Bronzing powder can work as an overall tint of colour to the face, or used on the cheekbones can give great definition. Apply with a large brush for sheer colour, or use a smaller graduated brush to define your cheeks.
- Apply lip pencil before and after lipstick application so you can achieve a precise clean finish and correct shape if necessary. Use a nylon brush to apply lipstick evenly and to the full extent of the lips. Use a single tissue to blot colour and then re-apply colour for long-lasting wear.

Anthony Murray on Hairdressing

Anthony Murray Hair Salon Group, Crowe Street, Temple Bar, Dublin
Irish Icon Hall of Fame Award 2006
Three-time winner of the Frank Hession Stylist Award

Of course, I would say this as I am a hairdresser but I genuinely think hair and make-up are such important things to get right on the day that is in it. After all, the bride is hiring a professional photographer for a day, possibly the only day of her life she will invest so much money, so it is essential that the bridal party look and feel their best.

You should spend on *yourself* as much as you can. Hair and make-up are two things that have to last all day. There are so many areas you can cut back on with a wedding, so much money wasted on non-essentials when priority should really be given to the bride and groom looking and feeling great . . . to feel your best throughout the day and to be happy looking at the photographs for years to come.

You see a bride with a fantastic personality, a fabulous dress but then the hair, it just doesn't go, it just doesn't match. While we do traditional styles we usually try to finetune the style in line with the personality of the bride, the dress and her hair type.

Imagery is key. Look at hairstyles you like and cut out pictures. This will help you and your hairdresser come up with the perfect look.

The period before the wedding is the time to decide on your look, not the day of the wedding. We do a serious amount of wedding work here in the salon so I can advise, from experience, that a trial is essential so you can decide properly what you do and don't like and it allows you time to decide and change things. It is important to take time to decide what style suits the dress, the hair type, the bride's personality. It is also important if you want to get colour done or colour sorted out, use a hair piece, extensions, whatever you need.

Ideally the bride will book her dress fitting and trial on the same day. You can get the wrong impression of the style if you are wearing jeans and a T-shirt; it can look very fussy. It is important to see everything fit together. So if you can, attend your hair and make-up trial in the morning and then see it all together in the afternoon, with shoes, hair, jewellery and the dress combined. In its full context you can get a good sense of how it will or will not work.

A hairdresser can call out to the house on the morning of the wedding. The call-out fee is money well spent, as it frees up the bride considerably on the morning, saving time on parking etc. If this can be arranged for the morning of the wedding, where the bride is in a quiet room away from bridesmaids complaining about tan on their elbows or the doorbell ringing, it can be very calming.

I have seen home-done bridesmaids' hairstyles in past weddings that simply don't work. I would stress that if a bride is going to have someone come do her hair, if she can at all she should have the bridesmaids' hair done too. If this is too expensive she should ask her bridesmaids if they would pay or at least meet half-way (or just have one bridesmaid!). But trials for bridesmaids are costly and not required. Just consider and discuss styles in advance, which will save time on the day.

I notice a lot of brides don't want to be perceived as bossy. I hear brides all the time saying they don't want to push anything, that it is up to their bridesmaids what they want. I sometimes feel the need to tell the bride that it is her call — she has bought the dresses and if she has certain ideas about how she would like the bridal party to look on the day, she should direct the bridesmaids. Officially it is their job to assist the bride and to meet the demands of the bride. If the bride would prefer they had their hair done professionally they should agree. If the bride is clear on what she wants it makes life easier for everyone.

Most guys just go to the barber the morning of the wedding, maybe for a hot shave. Some girls ask (demand!) that their fiancés make more of an effort on the day that is in it, more styled or highlights. Some guys are very into looking after themselves, so fair play to them, they are working to pay for this wedding so it is important. But mostly guys are happy with a trip to the barber.

Tips on styling depend on your hair and so are very individual, so speak to your hairdresser.

Price range Expect to pay up to €400 depending on numbers, home visit fee, trials etc. To me as a hairdresser I think this is money well spent, to look brilliant, all day. One final thing — my personal view is that it is the *bride and groom's* day, then the *mothers'* and then the *bridesmaids'.* So if you have someone coming to the house, and time willing, it is nice to treat the mammies to a blow dry too!

⌔ Webguide

barnardos.ie
bridalsales.ie
bridalshoes.co.uk
bridesave.com
buyandsell.ie
carnmeal.com
diamond.ie
diamondsandgoldireland.com
dreambridal.ie
e-weddingbands.com
eveningcourses.ie
face2.ie
faux.uk.com
glamgal.com
gownsales.com
groups.yahoo.com/group/leinsterfreecycle
hillcrestbridal.co.uk
houseofbrides.com
jumbletown.ie
lantz.ie/accessories
ncad.ie
netbride.com
nodirtygold.org
organicsilks.co.uk
oxfamireland.org
rkbridal.com
silverchilli.com
theweddingshop.ie
touchwoodrings.com
weddingsonline.ie/discussion
xe.com

Wedding Styles

Chapter Fourteen

Flowers and Decorations

Creating atmosphere on the day is easily done with a little time and effort. It doesn't have to cost the earth either. Brightening up the church or registry entrance with flowers or potted plants, adding ribbon to the seating area or some candles on the altar, centre arrangements on your dinner tables — every detail will combine to set the scene for a wonderful day. If you are using a non-traditional reception venue, such as renting a room in an unusual public building, then you will probably need to put more thought into decorating.

For weddings, flowers are the most popular way of decorating buildings (and people!). Florists are skilled professionals in their craft and are an enormous help with ideas and designs for your day. You may want your day to fit within a theme, be it a subtle colour scheme or an all-out Victorian style wedding. With so many wonderful ideas to choose from, this should be an enjoyable aspect of planning, a time when you can let your creative side see the light of day perhaps.

Remember, flowers and decorations are only one aspect of a relaxed, fun-filled day and can be enhanced by music, good food and conversation. If decorating does not interest you and begins to cause you stress, then remember there are always easier ways to do things, you don't have spend hundreds or go crazy with bows and balloons for your day to be special.

☼ First Decisions

Budget Depending on what flowers you choose and the florist you choose, prices will vary significantly. It is hard to give the cost of an average wedding, with some couples eager to dress every available surface in sprawling ivy and dozens of roses, while others are happy with a couple of neat displays at the entrance. A single rose carried down the aisle will cost you as little as €1 and a large bouquet filled with exotic flowers flown in from Thailand could cost three figures. So it is really best to phone around. Make an appointment to chat with your florist and she or he will work within your budget. When looking at price lists, remember you are not just paying for flowers but for the hours it takes to combine them perfectly, store them and assemble them on the day. At the same time, shop around to be sure you are getting a good deal. Clever positioning and using displays of varying heights can create a feeling of lots of flowers, even when there are not. If you have a large job on your hands, such as decorating your reception venue as well as the ceremony space, it is even more important to get good value for money.

Research Once you are clear on your budget you should then start to look into what you can get within your budget. Chat to a few florists and see what each discussion comes up with. If you are not sure you are getting value for money you should log on to wedding message boards to investigate what other brides are paying. Working creatively and imaginatively within your budget is essential, so you will need a skilled florist. If you are reasonably flexible and accept the limits you are working within, you shouldn't find it too hard to maximise impact on a much smaller budget. This should be an enjoyable experience, enjoying a few cups of coffee flicking through those glossy flower magazines. For inspiration, an excellent web resource to start with is *flowers.org.uk*, the website of the UK Flower Association. You will find most flower shops have websites too. You will probably love everything, but you will have to eventually narrow it down!

Using flowers in season can reduce the bill considerably. Exotic flowers flown in from faraway shores are obviously going to be more expensive than the daffodils growing up the road. Some flowers have a short season and are very expensive to source out of season, while others — thanks to breeding and growing techniques, coupled with imports from overseas — are available all year round. Generally it is best to keep within season if you need to keep within budget. Flowers that are in season are more affordable. See the table at the end of this chapter. While most popular bridal flowers are available year-round, some traditional ones — for example, peonies and lily-of-the-valley — can be difficult to find and expensive out of season. Seek your florist's advice before deciding on your flowers.

Simplicity with flowers can be more stylish than large, over-the-top displays. It has the added advantage of being a lot cheaper! Many florists express a preference for flowers in their natural state, combined simply rather than teased and packed together. Simple, well-placed arrangements can brighten up a room as much as some of the more elaborate alternatives. Simplicity can carry through to the bridal party. At a recent wedding I attended, the bride chose to carry a single rose walking down the aisle. This looked as beautiful as some of the most intricately (and expensively) designed bouquets I've seen in the past. A bride carrying one perfect rose down the aisle can concentrate on redirecting her budget into some show-stopping church decorations for the guests to enjoy. Remember also not to dismiss **'common'** flowers. The simplicity of a daisy ring in spring brings wedding church scenes from English heritage films to mind — Victorian brides with their wildflower posies. With a little imagination and skill, common flowers can upstage the most expensive roses!

If you are using a florist near your church or venue this can be an advantage as they may have pictures of previous work in your locations or at least some photographs of the displays they offer.

Location

Ceremony

It is wise to check with the Altar Society of the parish or the registrar as regards the do's and don'ts in the ceremony space. You might also find out there is another wedding on that day or the day before and you could use this to your advantage. In a small church or room the understated elegance of a delicate, well-placed display can look better, at a third of the price, than a large sprawling display. Similarly, in a large cathedral or town church focus should be on a doorway display to greet your guests are they arrive and perhaps some pretty pew ends to lead them to their seats. After this, let the building do the impressing!

Reception Venue

Although minor in comparison to good food and wine, centrepieces and room decoration should be an important factor when choosing your venue. The emphasis hotel staff place on making the venue look perfect for your day is a good indication of their respect for the occasion and dedication to making it perfect. If you have booked a beautiful venue, remember the currency you already have in terms of wow factor. If you are looking for a beautiful venue try and find a function room with windows; it is such a pity to get married in a beautiful hotel on a summer's day, only for everyone to be inside a windowless room. No chandelier can replace the sun shining through the window. It is a good idea to visit your venue to see the room prepared for a wedding. If you are a little disappointed, remember that you can chat to the hotel florist and suggest something different for your day, or you can add to the display easily, which could make all the difference.

■ **Arranging venue displays** Be sure to visit the room and walk around it. Don't depend on a well-taken photograph in a brochure; it could be years out of date. Think how the centrepieces or garlands will suit the room. If you have your heart set on soft pink flowers but the carpet in your reception room is a patterned red, you may need to re-think your colour scheme. If your venue is modern and minimalist, delicate country flowers in pastel shades could easily look out of place. The decision to do your own centrepieces, or pay a florist to do it, should not be made lightly. If there are already centrepieces on offer, consider adding to them rather than redecorating the entire room. This will save you a lot of money, but more importantly, it will save you the stress of arranging for a room to be decorated on the day of your wedding.

- **A blank canvas** If you are renting a hall for your wedding and starting with a blank canvas, the task ahead will feel quite daunting even for the most industrious, particularly if you have never done this before. Before you begin, ask the owner about previous events held in the room, and look for a phone number of someone who held an event there as you can be sure there are photographs of the room, and you can get a feel for how others managed. At the same time, simplicity often works well in decorating a room. In a room with high ceilings and large windows, wallpaper or paintings you might need nothing more than some white tablecloths and candlesticks.

> **Hiring a professional**
>
> Again, depending on your budget, if you have a large room that needs serious decorating and you don't know where to start, or you don't really fancy dealing with it yourself, you might consider having a professional come in the morning of the wedding. For about €500 an event management company will decorate your venue, provide tablecloths, centre displays, chair covers. This could be cheaper and a lot less hassle than trying to do it yourself.

☺ Self-sufficient

Flowers – To DIY or not to?

Our grandmothers' generation probably chat about making their own bouquets, perhaps even picking the flowers the morning of the wedding! You may not want to go as basic as that with things but if you do, be prepared to do a lot of practice in advance! It is often recommended by florists *not* to take a risk on doing your own bouquet, considering the unpredictability of flowers, the assembly time and the skill required. The romantic idea of picking wildflowers from a meadow and having a wild bouquet may not work out quite as romantic as you hope, with sore hands from putting it all together, possible seeds shedding all over the place and spiders hanging from them! So make sure to test the idea a few times before the day. Of course, you wouldn't have to have everything done by a florist; you can get the bouquets done professionally and there are some safer options when using flowers to decorate your venue, for example, for a modern, stylish look at your reception you could use glass vases with the tall purple pom-pom-like alliums. Have a look at this example in the wedding section of *flowers.org.uk* in the wedding section (summer 2006).

Risk Taking

While I have recommended here that you use a florist for flowers, you might not be that bothered and be happy to take a risk. If you do, always have a back-up plan in the form of a candle or a horseshoe to carry down the aisle. Also remember doing your own arranging might save on florist labour expenses but you will still be paying for the flowers, foliage and a little for the service, and you will also have to arrange for delivery and set-up. If you are that way inclined, now would be a better time than any to take up a new hobby and be sure to do it right. (See *eveningcourses.ie*.) If you can't afford a class, at least invest in a good 'how-to' video.

Finding Flowers

You could order your flowers from a flower shop when making your own arrangements. This way you can get advice from the florist about what to do to ensure it works out. There is also the possibility of visiting flower markets to pick flowers yourself, for example the Smithfield flower market in Dublin. If you are worried about the shelf-life of the flowers, keep in mind that most commercially grown flowers will last at least a week if treated right. Commercially grown flowers are specially treated after cutting, which means they will last longer than varieties cut from the garden. 'Conditioning' is the term florists use to mean getting the flowers ready for arranging. By following these few simple steps you can get extra life and pleasure from your flowers. But remember these tips are for day-to-day flower arrangements so to be sure you should have a few trial runs with your wedding flowers.

Season I would say to your readers that one of the strongest pieces of advice we give to brides here in the UK, particularly those working to a tighter budget, is to buy in season. You can get tulips in June and peonies in January if you really want — but they will be flown in on request from the Southern Hemisphere at great expense. Far better to choose flowers that are in season, our website can advise brides on what is flowering when.

What we don't advise brides on a budget to do is arrange their own flowers. Firstly they will have to buy wholesale quantities of flowers when they might only want two or three stems of something. They will have to condition them (strip all the leaves off, cut the stem ends, put them in water and flower food) — and green scratched hands are not attractive in the wedding photos. Also for some flowers they will have to judge how far in advance to get them and how to prepare and store them (the right cool or warm temperatures) so the flowers are all open on the wedding day, as most flowers will be sold in tight bud which won't look as good in the photos. If it is a hot day, or a particularly cold one, some flowers may suffer; and florists will know how to cope with this. A florist will be able to help brides with all these aspects and will know how to prepare flowers so they are open at the right stage, and so they last through the ceremony looking fresh. We have even known some families with no flower experience, elect to dress the reception hall including attaching flowers to the beams of the roof. This is something that florists do regularly and they know the mechanical tricks to ensure the flowers stay secure. I dread to think what would happen if parts of the arrangement started dropping off onto the guests during the meal ... all to save a bit of cash! It's tiring and stressful enough getting married, without doing your own flowers. Most brides wouldn't make their own wedding dress from a pattern and a length of fabric with no dressmaking training; or bake and ice the cake themselves if they had never cooked before ...

Top Tips for Cut Flower Care

The UK Flowers & Plants Association recommends the following simple tips, to ensure that your flowers last longer and look lovelier:

1. Make sure vases are very clean.
2. Use fresh lukewarm water with commercial cut flower food added.
3. Strip all leaves below the water level.
4. Take at least 3 cm (1 inch) off all stems, making a slanted cut with a sharp knife or very sharp scissors.
5. Avoid direct sunlight, heat, or draughts which can shorten flowers' lives.
6. Keep flowers away from fruit and remove faded flowers as they occur.
7. Top up the water regularly and add flower food in proportion.

Do

1. Buy flowers from a reputable outlet, and choose blooms with firm petals or with buds that show a degree of colour to ensure the flowers will develop fully.
2. Ensure the flowers are well wrapped for protection and, if the flowers are to be kept out of water for some hours, ask the florist to cover the stem ends with damp paper, or even to 'aquapack' them in their own water 'pod'.
3. Ask for cut flower food if it is not already supplied. This contains the correct ingredients to a) feed the flowers properly, b) keep bacteria at bay (which blocks the stem and stops water uptake), c) encourage buds to open, d) lengthen the life of the flowers. Snipping the corner off a one-dose sachet and adding it to the vase water is simple and effective — and scientifically tested to make your flowers last longer.
4. Use lukewarm water — there's less oxygen in it, and it helps prevent air bubbles in the stem that will block water uptake. It also encourages some flowers to open up. The only exception to this is spring bulb flowers like daffodils and tulips, which prefer cold water.
5. Use thoroughly clean vases — bacteria kills flowers.
6. Cut stems at an angle. This gives the stem a bigger area to take up more water, and stops it resting on the bottom of the vase and sealing itself.
7. Follow the care and conditioning stages outlined below to prolong the life and beauty of the flowers.

Don't

1. Smash or pierce the stems, or use blunt scissors, as this destroys the water vessels and inhibits water uptake, and causes bacteria to multiply more quickly and over a larger area. It also causes the flower undue stress which shortens its life.

2. Mix daffodils and narcissi with other flowers. They emit latex from their stems when cut, which is known as 'daffodil slime', and shortens the life of other flowers. Keep daffodils alone in vases, or use the special bulb cut flower food which makes them safe to mix with other flowers. You can place the daffodils in a bucket of water for at least 12 hours on their own and then arrange them with other flowers, making sure you do not cut the stem again.

3. Put flowers near ripening fruit — it releases tiny amounts of ethylene gas which prematurely ages flowers. Dying flowers do the same so always remove them from the vase.

4. Place flowers in a draught which chills the flowers, or in bright sunlight which encourages bacteria to breed. Keep them away from over-warm central heating.

5. Put copper coins, aspirin, lemonade, or bleach in the water. They're popular tricks but they don't work, and they can't feed your flowers adequately. Homemade formulas are messy, time-consuming and do more harm than good.

> **Ivy**
> Using freshly cut ivy from your garden as a filler for pew ends or at the base of candles is an inexpensive option and will look great combined with lilies and tied together with raffia. For lots of decorating accessories visit *carnmeal.com*.

🕐 Good Timing

Winter wonderland An already decorative time of year all round is obviously Christmas. If you are getting married in a church at Christmas the church may already be decorated. Ask your celebrant or altar committee what the church will look like then; will there be a Christmas tree and decorations? You might only need to add some holly to your pew ends and a couple of white trees at the entrance.

Flowering bulbs Purchase your centrepieces from a garden centre the day before a wedding. Amaryllis, narcissus, and hyacinths often cost less than regular flowers and are dramatic rising from a layer of stones set in clear containers. Check out the range in Marks & Spencer, Dunnes Stores or even Tescos. Your local garden centres should also be of great assistance with this.

 **Clever Tips**

The UK *Wedding Flowers* magazine is worth a look for ideas, with pages of beautiful arrangements. A few cut-outs will really help your florist get a feel for what you want. *Wedding Flowers* magazine is available in Eason's.

Frills White ribbon on the church gate, a red carpet, tulle bows at the end of seats, candles on windowsills and ivy trails hanging from pew ends. Mixed berries, pinecones (for winter), and other economical non-floral embellishments will combine beautifully with your flowers, helping create the overall look you are after. You can buy white lantern centrepieces on eBay for as little as €10 plus postage.

Balloons often evoke ideas of kids' birthday parties and can look tacky hanging from lights at weddings. But don't be so quick to reject the idea; some plain white or silver or gold balloons really can look stylish if nicely displayed along with flowers. Three white balloons tied on long silver strings rising from a weight on the floor (a silver horseshoe perhaps) can brighten up a dull bathroom where guests will be in and out all day. Or frame an unsightly fire exit. They can also be used to direct guests towards the room if it is in a complicated building.

Feathers are a wonderful item to decorate with: mallard's quill, pheasant feathers, teal duck feathers, French partridge feathers, and the beautiful spotted guinea fowl feather to name but a few. You can purchase feathers in most craft stores and online on eBay too.

◖ Something Different

Diamante into the bouquet This is my personal favourite for jazzing up a simple posie. Particularly beautiful set against darker flowers, this can make the tiniest gathering of red roses, in a lace bow, look like something from Tiffany's window. This can complement some beautiful diamante hairclips in your hair or crystals on your veil.

Silk The idea of artificial flowers probably conjures up images of cheap department store canteens or old graves. But be prepared to be surprised. Many brides talk about how delighted they were with their silk flowers — not a single guest noticed that they were not real. As a bouquet, they are a much cheaper alternative to fresh flowers, especially if you sell them on after. If you have decided in advance the type of flower you want, this should be considered when choosing a florist. Some florists offer a wide range of silk flowers, others none at all. You can buy flowers on eBay or try *hibiscusflorals.com* or *wedideas.com*.

> You could buy some latex cala lilies which look very realistic and surround them with foliage. A bride that did this commented on a message board that they 'were so much less hassle as I got them two weeks before and I still have them now! No one guessed they weren't real and wouldn't believe me when I told them. They were about €5 per flower.'

Crystal bouquets A more recent trend in weddings is to give flowers a miss and hold Swarovski crystal bouquets. To see if this is for you, visit *caradandesigns.com* or, of course, eBay will have them.

Ditch petals If you want something different I would recommend *not* scattering petals on tables. Before this, silver and gold confetti shapes were very popular. Like the two chocolate box favours, these finishing touches are now quite common at weddings so if you prefer to look different, do something new.

Let your imagination run wild Buy a white tablecloth and try it out at home. Look at the displays in department stores such as Brown Thomas and see if anything stirs your imagination. For example, bowls filled with seasonal fruits from a farmers' market can take the place of expensive floral presentations. Fruit or berry baskets, in the right setting with the right napkins, or some chair covers perhaps can really look fantastic. Or you can buy frosted drinking glasses very cheaply in the pound shop or even department stores. Wrap the glasses in a little organza ribbon with perhaps some coloured sand at the bottom and pop in a little nightlight — they look really special. Enjoy trying out ideas and discovering the many books in your local library on table decorating and wedding flowers.

🍃 Eco-Ethical Eye

Request Irish-grown flowers Order locally grown, seasonal flowers for your wedding. Ask the local florist about local growers; find out what is in season. Remember the less transport the less carbon miles. Even sticking with our neighbours can make a difference: see *englishplants.co.uk*.

Pesticide-free alternatives Look for organically grown flowers that were grown sustainably.

Grow your own! Have you got twelve or even six months left before your wedding day? Why not grow your own table arrangements! Choose native Irish species, or consider cultivating wildflowers. Living flowers are perfect as they are not cut and cultivated simply to be thrown away (or transported elsewhere). They can be given as meaningful gifts afterwards, or planted in your garden as a fragrant reminder of your day. If you have less time, don't panic — support small businesses by buying living flowers locally.

Share your happiness Ask a friend to take any leftover displays or bouquets to a nearby nursing home or to decorate a long-forgotten grave.

🐭 Webguide

caradandesigns.com
carnmeal.com
englishplants.co.uk
eveningcourses.ie
flowers.org.uk
hibiscusflorals.com
theknot.com (The excellent wedding bios on this site show some great DIY bouquets and ideas for the aspiring florist.)
wedideas.com

✳ ✳ ✳

Appassionata: Inspiration In Full Bloom

Ruth and Ultan from Apassionata Flowers, Sandymount, Dublin 4
appassionata.ie

Wedding party flowers

The bride will have the larger bouquet; however, the bouquet should work in proportion and colour to the bride and her dress. (All bouquets used in magazine or book shots are oversized for photographic impact!) Also, think about the photos — a colour too similar to the dress will blend in; the softer, really delicate flowers will fade after a few hours.

Bridesmaids can either have a smaller version of the bride's bouquet, hold a bouquet in a colour to pick up a detail of their own dress or wear a wrist corsage — these are increasingly popular.

Flower girls are usually so young, so just give them the tiniest of posies or petals in a basket . . . they usually lose their flowers halfway up the aisle!

I always suggest simplicity is best for a **buttonhole** as men are unused to having flowers so close to them! A single flower with a camellia leaf or sprig of rosemary looks fantastic against dark suits. It's always good to suggest to a bride that the groom and groomsmen have a female to oversee the buttonhole pinning as they can be attached in funny ways if the guys do the pinning badly! Often these aren't noticed until the wedding photos are developed! Politically, check with the mums and dads as to whether they would like to have a buttonhole or corsage — we have often turned up with the bridal party flowers to find an upset parent as they were not included in the mix.

Timing

When a bride has settled from the celebrations of getting engaged, she is usually subject to everyone telling her that she needs to get everything booked straight away. Whereas this may be true with a venue, it's not necessary with a florist unless you are getting married at Christmas time. We often get harassed newly engaged brides ringing in a panic, and my answer every time is to pencil the date in and then to tell them not to come back to me until they have their own dress sorted. This is because everything is so new at this stage and they have no focus on what they would like flowerwise.

Forget the price list!

We also constantly are asked for a price list or brochure. As every bride is different and would like different flowers in different styles, and as every church/ceremony and reception setting can vary so much, I can't offer a price list. Also, some people want everything filled with flowers, others just want the church or ceremony and the bridal party covered and some just want flowers for the bridal party — individuality reigns in weddings!

The best thing to do is to meet the florist, talk to them about your ideas and ask them for a proposal with approximate costings and then see how you would like to work your flower budget. If your budget is tighter than you thought originally, your florist should be good at guiding you to where you can best spend your money, i.e. you probably don't really need all those pew ends or all your family don't need to wear a buttonhole etc.

Don't be suspicious

You shouldn't need to be suspicious either of your florist. Increasingly on wedding chat rooms and in articles, brides talk about a florist ripping them off and charging horrifically for their wedding flowers. If your florist is good, they will work to your budget, the price offered basically accounts for your flower choice and the work involved with creating the beautiful wedding pieces, plus VAT has to be added on and included in the price. If you don't feel secure in your relationship with your florist, as long as you have no deposit paid, you are better to move on — brides need to remember that the wedding day is their day and that it should not be dominated by the florist telling them how it is. There have been many times I have created bouquets for bridal parties that I might not necessarily like but if the bride really would like it, I will create it and make it as beautiful as is possible.

The first visit
Once the dress has been chosen, the church or blessing space chosen, the venue or marquee confirmed, then it is time to visit your florist. If you would like rooms or ceremony spaces dressed in a particular way, it is worth it to have your florist recce them with you. Otherwise, if distance is a problem, you could take good digital photos (ask the florist what they are looking for) and email them to the florist so that they have a good idea of how to work the flowers to suit.

Images, fabric swatches, textures, colours and any cut-outs are good things to bring to your flower meeting. This gives your florist a good indication of the style and colour you would like to base your wedding flowers on. The first meeting can take an hour and it is good to meet in their shop/studio as any florist will have loads of images, references and obviously flowers to illustrate styles and flower types.

The church/ceremony space
Decide if you would like the space dressed. This might sound mercenary but if budget is a consideration, you are only usually in the church or space for an hour and on the day you won't notice the arch or bay trees or massive pedestals as you will be so concentrated on going up the aisle to meet your future husband. You could just use candles and ivy from a garden wall to dress the church, which looks fabulous.

Whatever you decide, keep these flowers fairly traditional-looking, as a very contemporary style really jars in these buildings. Whatever you decide, always check with the priest what he will allow in the church. Your vision of how the church should look and his sensibilities do not always meet eye to eye.

The venue
Usually, tables are dressed with a floral centre — your florist can create flowers to suit the venue and the vibe of your wedding day. You can play with different ideas here, i.e. if your favourite colour is pink, then use that as a base; if you love a funky, structured look, then here is the place to do it.

We are often asked about creating napkin ties with flowers attached. These are a lovely idea but take hours to make up. A venue will often throw in table flowers as part of their wedding package – a good tip here is to try and tie the flowers in with the look and feel of your day so that you don't turn up and the standard old lily is sitting pretty in a stem vase. Most venues are fairly accommodating on this.

Thank You Mum bouquets
This is a funny one. Whereas it is such a lovely idea to thank your mums on the day and give them flowers, more often than not, the mum has nowhere to put the flowers and when we clear a wedding the next day, we often find the poor bouquets left lopsided in a corner. A suggestion here is that the venue manager puts them in a cool room for you after they have been presented.

Ultimate no-nos
There are several no-nos: mixing red and white together, putting too many colours and flower types in one small bouquet, long shower bouquets which look out of proportion with current wedding dress styles, carnations and chrysanthemums as flowers to use – the most important thing in considering your wedding bouquet is to make sure the bouquet is in proportion to your body, i.e. if you are small and petite, don't have a huge dome of roses.

On a budget
It's good to think about where you really want the flowers to enhance, i.e. for the reception, drinks areas are always really busy with everyone greeting each other so flowers will probably be missed . . . If you would love nice table centres, use seasonal flowers with quirky ideas, e.g. small glasses with single blooms in them clustered around the table mixed with nightlights look sweet, small pots or vases with herbs or flowering plants in them look really special, they could have a ribbon or coloured string or fabric tied in a funky knot around them. Fishbowls with several flowers wrapped around the inside look really dramatic ... keep your personal flowers simple using one kind of flower or have a wrist corsage for the bridesmaids and then just one flower head for buttonholes.

A few ideas about seasonal flowers
Summer Hydrangea, peonies – they come in so many fantastic colours, and peonies in particular get that ice-creamy look.

Spring Wonderful for flowers with sweetpea, lilac, ranunculus in light springy colours.

Autumn There's a change in the natural colour palette here, with white eucharis, rusty hydrangeas and berries, and chocolate cosmos is fantastic and so pretty.

Winter Roses and ranunculus are the best to use here. Amaryllis are too big to hold in a bouquet.

Doing your own flowers

Having recently done my own flowers as a florist for my own wedding, I would advise not doing your own flowers. Luckily my mother had booked me in for a final manicure the afternoon before so that was my cut-off point; your hands need to look nice as there is so much focus on them the next day with ring viewing, photos etc. Florist hands get that cold red look and nails get ruined so this should dictate what to do.

If you are going to do it yourself, keep it very, very simple. I have yet to hear of a bride or family member who enjoyed doing the flowers at their own wedding. Your florist will get flowers at a much better rate than you, they can also find unusual shades and varieties much easier from their suppliers. If you do the flowers yourself, you will need adequate storage space and buckets, proper scissors, plenty of hands to help out and it just might be the last thing you would like to do on the day before you get married. I suppose it's a time versus cost factor: you probably won't save much money by doing the flowers yourself and you will spend time on it when you could have been having a nice walk or coffee with your folks!

Chapter Fifteen

Favours

A favour is a little surprise trinket next to your guest's plate. For anyone on a tight budget this is an unnecessary extra. It is not something that is expected at a wedding. You are much better channelling your money elsewhere. I have been to many weddings, including my own, where there were no favours and they were not missed. It can cost between €2 for your standard two-chocolate box, up to €6 for some of the more elaborate items on the market. For a medium-sized wedding this adds up quickly. Don't just purchase favours for the table because you think you should. Well-intended favours can often end up as dust collectors, if they are taken home at all. Staff at any hotel will tell you how many they put in the bin at the end of the last wedding meal. That said, if you have a really good idea and this is something that matters to you, it is a nice surprise for guests. And there are ways you can cut back.

Women only Let's face it, favours are a very female idea so why not just let your lady guests enjoy a favour. This will halve the bill.

Go online There are many wedding websites offering good value favours. If you are buying in bulk and the exchange rate is good you could really make a saving here by going further afield to the UK or the US. See Webguide.

Decoration If your table layout looks a bit dull, then favours are a nice way of brightening things up. Something very simple like as a sprig of lavender, or a beautiful place name can add to the colour of your table if you are decorating it yourself.

DIY party Make your own. Or have your own pre-wedding party with your friends and have everyone join in to make favours with you, be it iced cookies or simply wrapping ribbon around candles or the traditional bag of sugared almonds. *Diywedding.ie* stocks these little bags.

Edible The nicest favours are edible. A lot of couples leave a little box of chocolates next to the guest's plate. This is a nice (although very predictable!) idea. For a fresher approach why not ask for a silver tray of chocolates to be brought round with tea and coffee. Or gingerbread brides and grooms. You could make them in advance and freeze them. A few days beforehand you could ice and decorate them with friends. It would definitely be a talking point! You could even incorporate this activity into the day of your hen and mention to guests that the cookies are homemade by the girls (don't leave it too late on the day of your hen or you might find your friends getting a little too creative!).

Tickle the senses Cinnamon sticks or sachets of herbs with a nice recipe attached for your guest to try, makes a simple, tasteful gift.

Seasonal weddings Favours are excellent for themed weddings: little eggs on the side plate at Easter, a Christmas decoration attached to a place name ... something green for St Patrick's weekend. For February, do Valentine's chocolates; plastic pumpkins filled with jellybeans for autumn weddings.

From Russia with love My cousin lived in Russia prior to her wedding and on her wedding day she left little wooden boy and girl Russian dolls on each place setting. It was a beautiful idea, something significant from her past, and we hang the dolls on the Christmas tree every year! If you have an interesting background which suggests an idea, then go for it!

Merge your centrepiece and favours for maximum effect. Your florist can design floral centrepieces that complement the surrounding favours. You could also have each table do a little draw to take the centrepieces home (if they are yours). As an alternative to traditional flower centrepieces, group favours together on the table. Even if you spend a bit more on the favours themselves, you'll probably save overall.

Merge your place names with favours Using favours as items to hold the place names is also a handy merger. For example, a place name attached to an organza bag holding the treat.

The art of chocolate What I chose to do instead was purchase chocolates from my local chocolatier, Chez Emily. They were handed out on silver trays with the tea and coffee. They were fresh chocolates, and they went down a treat. It only cost me €60. See *chezemily.ie*.

Eco-Ethical Eye

The gift of a tree Or if you have access to a greenhouse you could gather acorns and pot them individually, one for each couple at your wedding. The gift of a tree to plant will definitely impress and get the conversation flowing when you unveil them. The planting of a tree per guest will offset the carbon emissions your wedding created.

A bar of **fairtrade chocolate** costs less than €1. This is a nice treat for guests to eat with their tea and coffee or to pop in their pockets for later.

Donate to charity Some couples choose to make a donation to their favourite organisation and print up a card or note to tell guests. This is a well-intended idea but it is nicer I feel to have something physical to show for the donation rather than a card telling the guest 'we donated to charity'. Perhaps a paws pin from the RSPCA (*rspca.org.uk*). If you have a charity close to your heart such as the Cancer Society of Ireland, it would be nice to purchase their daffodils if it is March.

Webguide

amnesty.ie
cakesandfavours.com
cancer.ie
carnmeal.com
chezemily.ie
diywedding.ie
fairtrade.ie
lantz.ie
rspca.org.uk
stick-n-mix.co.uk
traidcraft.co.uk
weddingcrafter.co.uk

Chapter Sixteen

Themes and Inspirations

You have probably started reading this chapter in anticipation of a laugh, but although some of the ideas here may not suit everyone, you might be surprised at how interesting others are. You may lack confidence about going with a full theme in case people will find it tacky, forced or plain silly. But keep an open mind; themes do not have to be full-on theatrical displays with guests being asked to dress up. They can be as subtle as a colour theme, a seasonal theme, a butterfly theme, incorporating a loved hobby or personal idea such as 'under the sea'. Themes create a talking point when guests enter the room, and can set the most traditional wedding apart from all the others. It is okay to be serious about getting married and serious about having some fun at the same time.

Simple A theme can be slipped through the invites, the bridal attire, the church flowers and venue decorations, perhaps even with some entertainment for your guests. Colour, for example, is an excellent way to tie the different elements of your day together. At Christmas the colours red and green would work beautifully, or you could have icicles hanging from the wine glass and silver ball place names, which can double as Christmas tree favours, holly centrepieces and lots of candles. At Easter over the white tablecloth you could put baby blue and pink gingham napkins, pastel-coloured chocolate egg favours and basket centrepieces. Even furry place names.

Origins You could celebrate your origins if you are from another country. This is a good way to make a traditional wedding a little more personal, by adding, let's say, a French twist or some Scottish shortbread and bagpipes.

Post-wedding party If you were married abroad and are having a return celebration, why not incorporate your wedding location into the party? Lay out your wedding album, put on your video and theme things up with a taste of the country you were married in. For example, a Caribbean wedding throws up so many ideas, bright colours, rum cocktails, some iron drums in the corner, you could even ask guests to dress colourfully with the men in Hawaiian shirts. You can find loads of adequately tacky themed accessories including colourful 'sandal candles' on *brideandgroomdirect. co.uk.*

> *theweddingshop.ie*
> Many of the items on this site are from Cox and Cox, which are a UK company selling beautiful decorations and wedding items. The prices on this site are excellent when compared to the prices on the Cox site. They have many little extras for decorations such as snowflake cookie cutters. Check out the beautiful butterfly garland, butterfly bubbles, rose petal soaps. This site will show you what you can do with a small budget to brighten up tables. See also *coxandcox.co.uk.*

Seaside theme Deep blue glass, sea shell centrepiece, fishing rod place names peeping out from the wine glasses.

Fairytale Some even go as far as having a full-on theatrical event such as a Cinderella type fairytale wedding. A large full wedding dress with sparkly tiara, bride and groom arriving in a horse and carriage, Cinderella glass slipper centrepieces (on sale on eBay!), large colourful displays in rich colours with gold candles on feather bases.

The ultimate chocolate theme! A chocolate theme is a classy, tasty and fun idea. Your bridesmaids could wear the brown dress style made famous by the Galaxy advertisements! Your invites could have a brown bow around a cream insert. Guests could be greeted on arrival by a chocolate fountain! They are expensive (about €5.50 per head) but if you are dedicated to a chocolate theme or simply want something exciting to greet guests at the hotel they really are great fun.

> 'We were so impressed with the chocolate fountain, as were all of our guests. It was such a massive hit with them and they were still talking about it when we got back from our honeymoon! As a number of our guests were non-drinkers I thought it would be nice to have a reception of a different kind for them when we reached the hotel. All our guests young and old loved it! It was worth every penny and I would highly recommend it if you are looking for something special and unique for your wedding day. The service was excellent and very professional and Tara was an absolute pleasure to deal with.'
>
> **Patricia and Sean**
>
> Contact Tara at *the-chocolate-fountain-company.com*. Based in Kerry.

Some chocolate inspiration:

cocochocolate.co.uk The boxes are beautiful for a centrepiece filled with chocolates to share with your table during coffee.

chocolate.co.uk The Chocolate Society website. They sell pricey but beautiful small heart boxes, eight pieces for £10.95, which are a beautiful centrepiece idea or for your tea and coffee reception. Check out their wooden box with chocolate squares. You could announce during the speeches that 'the youngest person at every table can keep the box'…now that'd be a conversation starter!

chezemily.ie My local chocolatier. Having had these chocolates at my wedding I can sincerely recommend them.

Eco Theme – Organic Weddings There is an entire website dedicated to organic weddings. It is US based: *organicweddings.com.*

Inspiration

During my research I came across many sites that are excellent sources of inspiration, for ideas on wedding styles, interesting wedding reports, alternative options and good sources of information.

http://bios.magnificentbliss.com Weddings are big affairs in America and brides often post all the ins and outs of their weddings on 'bio' pages. Here you will find a collection of brides' biography pages from various websites. The bios are rated, allowing you to have a peep at the best sites. There is a lot of madness, serious wedding planning, over the top ideas, as well as some excellent photographs and inspiration for your day.

xena-productions.com This is the site of wedding planner Tara Fay. The photographs of her creations might inspire you to be adventurous on your day.

theweddingshop.ie This site carries many beautiful, frivolous extras to add to your day. They stock beautiful decorations such as butterfly garlands and there are also some cute ideas for presents such as a flower girl memory book and the 'bridesmaid' T-shirt.

coxandcox.co.uk This UK shop sell some beautiful and some quirky products such as sparklers, fairy lights, interesting favours.

marthastewart.com This is the site of the ultimate domestic goddess Martha Stewart. Martha certainly knows how to dress a table or wrap a gift. You won't find too many budget savers here but the images are beautiful and should really inspire you.

weddingsbyfranc.com You may have seen the show on RTÉ and witnessed Peter Kelly's miracles! This man knows how to throw a party. His website is excellent too.

Webguide

brideandgroomdirect.co.uk
chezemily.ie
chocolate.co.uk
cocochocolate.co.uk
coxandcox.co.uk
http://bios.magnificentbliss.com
marthastewart.com
organicweddings.com
the-chocolate-fountain-company.com
theknot.com
theweddingshop.ie
weddingsbyfranc.com
xena-productions.com

Chapter Seventeen

Stationery

This is an area where you have lots of choice at all budget levels. It is certainly not an area to get stressed out about. For those of you with a very tight budget this is an excellent time to clear the kitchen table for an evening and get creative. You will be surprised how enjoyable hand-making your own invitations can be. You could spend up to €1,000 on wedding stationery packages including invites, mass booklets, thank you cards and menus, but the average price for a personalised package is between €300 and €600. However, nowadays with printers available in most homes and free computer downloads on many wedding websites you can source your own materials, design and print your stationery at home, at very low cost.

⚡ First Decisions

Invitations The cheapest option is buying **ready-made** invitations from high street stores. You just complete the names, date and venue by hand. This is the hassle-free option and there are many good quality and inexpensive varieties to choose from. For personalised invitations you can order bespoke designs from a professional stationery maker either in person or online. This is the most expensive option. For real savings on personalised invitations it is highly recommended to go the **DIY** route. More and more couples are making their own personalised invitations these days.

> I had my invitations designed as I wanted to incorporate a photograph from both our communion days onto the card. It was an idea I read about and I had my heart set on it. To do this in Ireland would be very expensive so I went with a company in London who were significantly cheaper at the time, *haveandhold.co.uk*. (My invitations are displayed number 4 in the yellow section.) As I spent more in this area than I had to, I saved by skipping RSVP cards, making my own place names, mass booklet covers and buying thank you cards in Eason's.

Remember you will only need to order one invitation per couple. For a wedding of 150 people you will probably need about 75 invitations allowing some spares for mistakes.

RSVP cards These are very much optional. Some people choose the added expense of putting stamps on them to encourage responses. However, if you are sending 75 invitations, this small gesture will cost you €36 in stamps. Save your money and just prepare yourself for the inevitable few chase-up phone calls. You can also provide an email address, house address and a phone number for RSVPs instead. I had most of my replies by email.

Booklet covers Again optional. It is an added expense to design booklets for a wedding. If you do have them there are plenty of ways to avoid overspending. If you are going with a package it will probably include booklet covers as part of the theme. If not, you can buy ready-made booklets off the shelf. Then there is the option of purchasing heavy paper and printing them yourself. For an even cheaper option why not print a summary of the mass on good paper, detailing just the highlights, staple it, roll it up and tie it in ribbon. A perfect scroll for your guests. If I was to do it again, I would choose a scroll as booklets are a lot of work.

Thank you cards Again, the more expensive option here is to order personalised thank you cards with your invites. You are much better off buying them in a department store or online.

Place names You can go with various options here. Some people incorporate the place names into a theme that you can brighten up the room with, let's say, pink feathers attached to the card. You can also buy purpose-made place names with detail such as gold edging. These place names can be very expensive. I bought plain name cards in a standard stationery shop (€2.50 for 150!). I stamped the edges with a flower stamp. I asked a friend to write the names out using calligraphy. There is also the fun option of using little clothespegs, which you can find in craft shops, to attach name tags to the edge of glasses or a napkin fan. Or, keeping things very simple, you could use card paper cut into shapes with the names written boldly in a vibrant ink colour.

You will need to use full names for your table plan, but you can use just first names on your place names — this is less formal and less time consuming too.

Pick 'n' mix For each item you can choose a different method. If you really want bespoke invites you can have your invites designed and buy everything else off the shelf.

☺ Self-sufficient

Invitations There are a range of packages available from many sources to make your own invitations that look handmade, *not homemade*. *Diywedding.ie* stock beautiful handmade papers, high quality cardstock and pressed flowers. The average price of a DIY Invitation Kit is just €1 per invite and none is higher than €2. This compares with €5–€8 per invite for pre-printed invitations. You can choose a DIY Invitation Kit. There are over eighty pre-designed kits that come with all you need to make them up. Each kit comes with a pre-formatted MS Word Template that you download directly to your computer. Then you just change the wording, print and go! The kits come with very detailed and foolproof instructions. All designs are customisable — you can change ribbon colours and types, envelopes and pressed flowers and embellishments. You can also shop by colour scheme or start from scratch entirely and design your own invitations. This allows you to pick and choose papers, envelopes, ribbons and other embellishments to design your own invitations. The site has a separate information resource centre to help brides with any questions or queries they may have. You can find lists of typical fonts and links to free font websites to download unique wedding fonts. There is information and explanations on all tools and adhesives used to make invitations and a section of free downloadable templates for laying out and formatting your invitations — takes a lot of the pain out of making your own!

> *diywedding.ie* The site also sells favour bags, ribbons, place cards, table confetti, decorations, mass booklet covers and photo albums. These are all priced very reasonably — cheaper than any bricks and mortar shop.

Stamps For my booklet, I bought a beautiful Victorian style stamp and some light decorative paper from a stationery shop. I used this stamp again when decorating the place names. Very cheap, but very stylish all the same! You can purchase some beautiful stamps from shops such as Daintree in Dublin or you can try online at *craftfactory.ie, craftsupplies.ie* or *daintree.ie*.

☼ Clever Tips

Using a designer While the DIY route for some is cheaper, it may not always be feasible for a couple to go that way due to time constraints. For example, Noreen Clifford of Clifford Designs in Cork designs and hand-makes invitations to order. She says that while some couples are of the opinion that their invitations set the opening scene for their wedding with a continued theme throughout, others think of them as just a piece of paper which tells guests when and where the wedding is on. She emphasises that for couples who are on a budget there are always ways to cut down the costs of their stationery, even when going with a designer. For example adding an email address to the invitation wording, instead of enclosing a reply card with stamp and envelope or choosing a cheaper style of paper for the insert. (See *clifforddesigns.ie*.)

High street Marks & Spencer have a beautiful range of wedding invitations. They also have a CD ROM (€5) you can use to personalise your own invitations. This is an excellent way of using your home PC to print what look like professionally made invitations. (See *marksandspencer.com*.)

Debenhams also have a good range of wedding stationery. (See *debenhamsweddings.com*.)

Some of the UK sites offer excellent value for money. For example *brideandgroomdirect.co.uk* will not only supply stationery, they also sell personalised napkins and novelty items.

Argos sell plain white cards of various shapes. They also sell handy cutting mats and tools for paper craft.

Incorporating photographs into your stationery

There are numerous online photograph albums with services to purchase cards and other stationery using your chosen photographs. The possibilities for creativity are endless. Have a look at the demonstrations on these sites to see just what you can do: *photobox.ie, google.ie/picasa*. This Google software is free to download and will allow you to crop photographs, make them black and white or sepia, and create collages. This is an excellent resource if you are doing your own invites and incorporating a photograph on to the front. A scene from your wedding on the front of your thank you cards is very easy to arrange and looks just brilliant if done well.

> You may save some money if you order your invitations from an out-of-home stationer. However, make sure that person has good references.

Non-wedding print companies are worth approaching if you have a document prepared for print such as your booklet. They will often do the job for you at a very reasonable cost.

> Photo storage and development sites:
> *pixdiscount.com*
> *shutterfly.com*
> *kodakgallery.eu*

Something Different

messageinabottle.com For a very small wedding why not have your message sent in a bottle!

Eco-Ethical Eye

Obviously the greenest way is to telephone or email your invites! But invitations are a wonderful opportunity to be creative and you wouldn't want to miss out on that. So if you are making your own and want to source paper from a sustainable resource, you will find that many stationery stores stock recycled paper or you could try *rps.gn.apc.org*, specialist suppliers of quality recycled paper, card, envelopes and recycled stationery products by mail order.

eco-wedding.com This website is dedicated to helping you plan your own economical and eco-friendly wedding.

Webguide

bonusprint.co.uk Online photograph storage and processing services
brideandgroomdirect.co.uk Shop
clifforddesigns.ie Invitation designer
craftfactory.ie Stationery supplies
craftsupplies.ie Stationery and craft supplies
daintree.ie Stationery supplies
debenhamsweddings.com
diyweddings.ie DIY stationery supplies
eco-wedding.com To plan your economical and eco-friendly wedding
google.ie/picasa Free photo editing software
haveandhold.co.uk Invitation designer
kodakgallery.eu Online photograph storage and processing services
marksandspencer.com
messageinabottle.com Alternative invitations
photobox.ie Online photograph storage and processing services
pixdiscount.com Online photograph storage and processing services
rps.gn.apc.org Specialist suppliers of recycled paper products
shutterfly.com Online photograph storage and processing services

Chapter Eighteen

The Car

Unless the hotel and church are very close together you can't walk it, so you need a car. Of course, there are some who arrive by helicopter, horse and trap or even the back of a JCB! The tradition of a couple not seeing each other the morning of the wedding harks back to the long-gone days of arranged marriages. Many couples today live together before marriage, some already have children and most have let go of or disagree with most past superstitions and traditions. Often, couples decide to spend the night before their wedding together, drive to the church together and some even walk down the aisle together! Not everyone agrees with being 'given away'. However, many couples still decide to spend the night apart and arrive separately by car.

☀ First Decisions

Firstly, do you have a friend or relative with a stylish car? Be bold and ask the small favour of borrowing their car for the afternoon of your wedding. All you will need to do is provide some nice white ribbon to decorate the car.

If you decide to hire a car for the day, do make it just one car and not the entire fleet. In the morning this car can make two trips to the church, transporting the bridesmaids and then the bride. After the church ceremony why not arrange to have a friend drive the bridesmaids to the venue?

How much you spend on transport varies hugely, depending on what sort of car you want or what sort of entrance you might want to make. The average cost to hire a car and driver for three hours' work on your wedding day is €350, although you can spend upwards of €650 for specialist vehicle hire. Clearly this is an area where many couples lose the run of themselves! We are talking about getting from A to B here, so if you can at all, save your budget for the many other much more important parts of the day.

> **Some questions to ask the hire company:**
> Can I use the same vehicle to pick up several people?
> Are the vehicles available to see prior to the wedding?
> How many passengers does each vehicle hold?
> Is the driver familiar with the area?
> What does the driver wear?
> Does the charge per hour begin when the car leaves the garage, or when it arrives at the first pick-up?

☺ Self-sufficient

Something borrowed The best way to be self-sufficient here is to use your own car, but if it is a little too rusty for your white dress you should try borrowing a friend's or family member's car, perhaps in lieu of a gift.

☀ Clever Tips

Go modern So you want to make a dramatic entrance? Maybe you fell in love with a 'classic' (read tacky) 10 mpg Rolls Royce at a wedding fair? Are you sure it won't break down on the way to the church? Why not go for the simple understated elegance of a new Mercedes for less than half the price of a gas-guzzling old heap? Your entrance will be just as stylish and certainly more comfortable.

Rent it Consider renting a luxury or unique vehicle and have your best man drive it. Budget, Avis and Enterprise Car Hire offer an E Class Mercedes for €120–€130 per day. Book well in advance and make sure the hire company knows this is for your wedding day. Some companies will not guarantee the car you specify, so ask nicely!

Thinking outside the box Some funeral directors also hire for weddings. Their rates are often extremely competitive. See table for price examples.

Price Examples

Supplier / Location	Variety of Car	Price	Mileage
Colliers, Bray, Co. Wicklow (Funeral Service)	Daimler (Dropping top) Landaulette	€300	+ €25/50 negotiable
Church On Time.ie Galway	Rolls Royce Mercedes	€370 €250	65c per mile (if more than 4 hours away 45c)
Hertz Rental	Silver E Class Mercedes	€120	n/a
Avis Car Hire	Silver E Class Mercedes	€123	n/a

For further details visit *goldenpages.ie*.

◖D Something Different

Helicopter This is definitely an exciting entrance. Obviously this is not the budget option but if this is your dream then go for it. You will arrive at your venue before any of your guests. You can't put a price on an hour together for a drink before the crowds arrive.

Horse and carriage Again this will not keep the budget down and is not recommended if it is a long trek to your venue. But for anyone looking for the ultimate fairytale entrance then this could be for you.

Eco-Ethical Eye

We all know the damage carbon emissions do to the environment. Check out exactly how much your journey will cause at *carboncalculator.com*. Shocked? Then walk it! Choosing a hotel near your church will also save on emissions from guests' cars travelling.

> If you decide to walk and are worried about rain, check 'Cupid's Brolly' out! Definitely good for a laugh. See *iwantoneofthose.com*.

 ## Webguide

carboncalculator.com What damage is your journey doing?
goldenpages.ie
iwantoneofthose.com Shop

Recording the Day

Chapter Nineteen

Photography

Photographers are skilled professionals, often self-employed with all the overheads that brings, but on an hourly basis a typical wedding photographer is up there with the country's best surgeons! On top of the price you will also often be charged hefty travel expenses for anywhere outside a five-mile radius of the studio. You will pay significant add-ons for further prints too. So be prepared for a shock when you start phoning around. Standard packages cost from €700 to €3,000 but be aware you probably still won't own the copyright or any of the negatives.

Of course, there are ways of saving some money here. And there are some reasonably priced packages out there too if you look a little harder.

☀ First Decisions

Scrap the album Many couples are now going for a photo-only package, or even a disk-only package. It is very easy to source high-quality wedding albums in the shops or online. By sourcing your own album you will avoid paying over the odds for similar albums from a photographer. By putting it together yourself you will also save on the mounting fee.

Attend a studio If you want professional photography on the day, one guaranteed shoot, but you are not prepared to pay the high prices, you could book to visit a photography studio on your way to the reception. For winter weddings this can take the worry out of searching for a good indoor spot for photographs. For a fraction of the price you will have professional photographs on the day. You can rely on your parents and guests for the rest.

> Be sure to buy high-quality albums that will preserve your photographs adequately.

☺ Self-sufficient

If professional photographs are not a high priority for you, or maybe like me the video matters more, then perhaps you could take a chance by asking on your invites that guests supply you with a copy of their photos. With digital cameras and budding photographers at every turn you are bound to come across some fantastic shots.

> *aspinaloflondon.com*
> Leather albums from €150
>
> *katespaperie.com*
> Italian albums from €180
>
> *newbridgesilverware.com*
> Silver-plated albums from €95

 # Clever Tips

Network Researching offers on message boards on the internet can be very helpful. You will regularly find brides referring to friends of the family, local start-up photographers offering great deals for photo-only packages. These people often work from home and do not have to sustain high overheads.

Negotiate Perhaps you only want formal shots at the church, and so you only need the photographer for before and after the mass. For reduced hours and reduced work you should be able to negotiate a good price.

Disposable cameras Many couples put cameras on the tables in their reception room with a note suggesting guests take photographs and return it. If done well, this can be an excellent idea. But remember to leave instructions, as guests may assume the cameras are a gift. It is also reasonable to suggest photographs of each other, the evening, etc. rather than 'hilarious' random pictures. You will after all be paying to develop the shots in the hope there are some good ones for your album.

Get it in writing Get your prices in writing so your services are not subject to the New Year price hike.

Student photography Although wedding photography is a skill in itself and if you want perfect shots you should hire a wedding photographer, for those of you who just want some nice pictures of the day and nothing too fancy why not check your local college for photography students. Contact the professors to see if they have a 'work for hire' programme and for a list of the best students to consider.

 WARNING

If good photographs mean a lot to you, you will need to be sure that they are in good hands. This is not an area to take a chance on anyone. Do not book anyone unless you have seen their previous work and you like it. Log onto *irishphotographers.com* and follow the tips for booking.

My photographer was terrible, the only bad thing that happened in the whole day. He was bossy and sent all my guests away from the church to the reception so they did not see me leave or get a chance for confetti. I would never have used him had I known that one of my guests, a close friend of mine, was taking better pictures than the photographer did! I would say that if you have any friends good at taking pictures and money needs to be saved, then don't bother with a professional photographer. With so many guests having digital cameras these days you can do your own album from the best shots.

Top tip: I was so happy I put disposable cameras on the tables at the reception. We got some brilliant photos.

Rachel, Galway

 # Webguide

aspinaloflondon.com Photograph albums
irishphotographers.com For tips on booking a photographer
katespaperie.com Photograph albums
newbridgesilverware.com Photograph albums

Chapter Twenty

Video/DVD

✺ First Decisions

Photography is still the first preference for most couples in recording the day. Although popular, professional video coverage is still not near as important for most people. Many couples are very happy to have friends and family take some footage on the day instead.

Shop around There are some good prices out there, especially from people new to the market. When you have viewed sample videos and have decided on the style of coverage you like best, then you can start the negotiation.

Part coverage If you would like the ceremony captured but the budget won't allow for further coverage, you should enquire about a **ceremony-only** deal. This is a recording of the guests arriving, the bride and groom arriving, the ceremony and some mingling outside the church.

Unedited If the ceremony-only price is still out of your price range, ask for *unedited* coverage. That way you can edit it yourself at a later date or ask a friend to do so.

 WARNING

Get your package in writing when you book. This will ensure no price hikes, no travel expense surprises.

You are *not* expected to provide a five-course meal for your videographer/s. However, it will probably be in the contract that you provide lunch. Venues are well used to dealing with this and can provide bar food or a one-course alternative. You may ask why you have to feed the videographer, after all your boss doesn't buy your lunch. However, the nature of the service requires that they give 100% for the entire time they are recording. It is therefore important that lunch is arranged in advance and they can record the speeches while eating themselves.

If you are using your own camera don't allow your camera to stray as it will inevitably end up sitting in a pool of cider. Your best bet is to give it to someone that doesn't drink or to arrange for the camera to go up to the room after the first couple of dances.

☺ Self-sufficient

Buy your own Maybe you resent spending €700 on this service and would prefer to buy your own camcorder and ask a guest to capture the day. Although it won't be nearly as high-quality as a professional, a guest with a steady hand might capture the day sufficiently for you. (See *pixmania.com*.) For camcorder reviews visit *which.co.uk*. The Which Guide offers a free two-week trial.

Hire a film student for a fraction of the cost of a professional. Even better, hire two students and you are bound to get enough good footage for editing into a wonderful video.

Tips for a good home-produced video

Have a look at some good wedding videos in advance and draw up a plan of what you would like shot. Arrange a good video camera and allocate jobs to reliable friends. Perhaps a family member not involved in the bridal party could cover the church shots, a pal could shadow the photographer during the photo session, and someone else could put the camera on a tri-pod for the speeches.

Key shots throughout the day
The church will be hard to cover properly without good equipment. If you are using a standard video it is best to stick to the entrance, the vows and the exit. Simple.

Shadow the photographer during the photo session before the reception.

Speeches Visit the venue in advance and pick a spot to put a camera on a tri-pod for the speeches. Ask a friend to keep an eye on the coverage.

Cutting the cake Tell the cameraperson to bully his way through the swarm of photographers to get a good shot of this.

Dance floor You will only need a short while of the first dance, combined with some dancing shots. This can be done in the first thirty minutes and then your amateur videographer can retire to the bar! The sound from a band rarely records well so it is best to edit over with similar music.

Novelty Pick a spot at the venue and ask some special guests to chat to the camera. The perfect time for this is between the meal and the dancing. Ask your groomsman to have a box of questions next to the chair: Tell me a story about Paul and Olivia, how did you meet? Do you have any embarrassing stories about the couple? Request that your guest answer at least two questions. This is comical when done in pairs.

🕐 Good Timing

As with everything, you have more bargaining power during the off season or on a quiet weekday.

There are courses in wedding videography in many colleges. Why not phone the teacher during term time and ask him to recommend a reliable student.

> My friends did a video of the wedding. I had two people at the wedding with home video cameras and I compiled the best bits from both – one was at the church before the wedding for the pictures of the nervous groom, and the other was at the house I was getting ready in. So we had some great pictures for the whole day. I used Unilead VideoStudio 8 SE VCD for creating my video. There are other really good programmes available, it just happened to be the one I had at the time. I found it more personal than having a stranger do it. Even though I did it myself, it is as good quality as some of the 'professional' videos I'd seen, better than some!
>
> **Rachel, Galway**

◀D Something Different

Do a video diary each Borrow two camcorders and video how you feel throughout the day, ask a groomsman and bridesmaid to catch you for five minutes at key moments of the day and record your thoughts. Even better, ask them to pass the video around (to steady hands!) to catch a few important guests' thoughts too. These thoughts could be combined later to music with your professional photos to make a beautiful collage.

> **Take mental pictures**
> Throughout the day, remember to stop, relax and take mental pictures of what's going on around you, smell the smells, taste the food, see the smiles on people's faces, see what people are doing, what they're saying. If you really look around, those memories are better than any expensive video or photos!

Stress-free diary Simply set up a camera in your bedroom, the diary room, the morning of your wedding and do similar in the bridal suite.

Sneak up throughout the day to chat to the camera about how things are going. Maybe ask your bridesmaids and groomsmen to join in.

Video editing software can be bought very cheaply or even downloaded for free (try *download.com*) if you want to cut and splice.

 # Webguide

download.com: for free software downloads
pixmania.com: good value equipment
which.co.uk: guide to purchasing a camcorder

Janet Beck and Ben Dolan on Video

Glass Eye Productions, Kilkenny, are a full-service multimedia production company based outside Kilkenny. While the company now specialise in corporate video and multimedia, founder Janet Beck spent three years covering the weddings of Ireland's rich and famous. Janet and Production Manager Ben Dolan offer a unique insight into the business of the wedding videographer.

For couples choosing a professional to cover their wedding, what would you suggest they look out for?

There are some things one should definitely watch out for when choosing a company or individual to record one's big day. The company history is important as is the background of the camera operator and editor. It is best to choose someone with a background in film or television, preferably with some documentary experience. A two-camera set-up is also preferable, as this will ensure seamless covering of the event — no breaks for changing tapes and/or batteries. Look at the company's or individual's promotional material, brochure, business card and especially their show reel. The quality of this material generally reflects the quality of their product; it should be slick, professional and creative. A wedding show reel should show an entire wedding (except perhaps the speeches to ensure discretion for the couple on the reel). The editing should be snappy and interesting to watch with no long-winded or repetitive shots. Ask to see additional samples if you are unsure. Testimonials from previous clients are also a good indication of what type of service you will receive. It is also a good idea to meet the camera person before booking as they will be with you for the entire day, and it is important you feel comfortable around them.

For someone sitting down to look at sample wedding videos for the first time, what would you feel indicates a good quality service and value for money?

The show reel is the videographer's best promotional tool. Look for things that you like in their other work, watch for their attention to detail, the quality of picture and sound, and if there is evidence of their having used imaginative ways to cover the important elements — church, reception, speeches etc. Camera work should be of a high standard, no shaky shots! Also watch for the quality of DVD menus and titles.

Points to look out for:

- Make sure there are no shaky shots. There is no excuse for this.
- Shots should always be clear and focused.
- Composition of shots should be interesting and framed correctly without the top of anyone's head cut off. A mixture of close-ups, wide, and creative shots makes a more interesting finished product.
- Watch out for yellow or blue tinted shots as this indicates the use of incorrect light filters.
- Sound quality should be clear with no hiss or other interference.
- Shots should be edited to suit the chosen music . . . not just a music track playing without any thought over the shots.

For a couple that simply don't have the money to hire a professional videographer would you have any advice or suggestions?

Many of the technical colleges now run media or film courses, so there are a great number of enthusiastic and talented students who need to make a bit of extra money, and many will have invested in or have access to all the equipment necessary to make a relatively decent quality video.

Another good alternative is the 'prosumer' — the video enthusiast who has equipment which, while not of a professional standard, can still produce reasonable results. Or perhaps hire a company to record part of the day that is most important to you and get the 'prosumer' to do the rest.

I was much happier with my video than my photographs, which cost twice the price. I can't understand why photographers charge so much and a video is usually much cheaper. Video coverage also involves skill and creativity, more time on the day capturing footage, and more time later editing. Why then does this service cost so much less than photographers?

This is something which I have been discussing with a colleague who is in the process of planning her own wedding, and it does seem that costs across the board have increased by up to 100% in the last five years and by 300–400% over a ten-year period. Photography seems to be a perfect case in point — the same photographer had increased their fee from €800 to €1,500 in five years; surely the cost of processing film cannot have increased by that much! The truth is that processing costs have increased but with most photographers having switched to digital this really should not be a factor, so they really do seem to be charging whatever the market will bear. A sensible piece of advice is to shop around and always ask people to justify their cost if the same service is available elsewhere for less.

Further Afield

Chapter Twenty-One

Getting Married Abroad

More and more Irish couples are choosing to relocate their wedding entirely. For some, the appeal is getting away for a simple relaxed ceremony, for others the lure is warmer climes that can fulfil the dream of an outdoor celebration. Two of the main reasons people are choosing to marry abroad are (a) less expense and (b) less stress.

Expense How much you save depends on your choices. One immediate saving is made through combining your wedding and honeymoon. The wedding and the wedding party are usually smaller with the savings that brings. Choosing a country where goods and services are more affordable means you have less money worries than the average bride and groom. In terms of the ceremony there are many more options abroad than in Ireland: a civil ceremony on the beach, a little white chapel in Cyprus or perhaps exchanging vows while floating above the clouds in a hot air balloon!

Stress Although getting married abroad does require meticulous planning, it can eliminate some of the stresses of a large traditional wedding. With probably less money worries to contend with, the day itself is often much more relaxed for the couple, in beautiful intimate surroundings, enjoying the best of local food and wine in the company of loved ones.

This chapter will help you to decide whether this option is for you and if so, it will provide you with some ideas on getting started on planning a wedding far away.

⚡ First Decisions

Pros of a wedding abroad

Size It is the perfect way to have a small wedding.

Guests Announcing a wedding abroad is not so daunting if you remember that with enough notice most people are delighted to plan next year's holiday around your destination. If you provide clear directions regarding airlines, pricing and accommodation to your guests, they can realistically tell you if it is something they can do.

Weather An outdoor wedding is a definite possibility in many locations where you can be confident of a dry day at the very least.

Extended event These weddings usually turn out to be much more extended events. Guests will usually 'make a trip' out of it and after sharing the day together they often stay around for some sightseeing. It is a great opportunity for both families to get to know each other, especially if they are staying in the same place.

Pre or post wedding party If you worry that important people can't make it, people who are buying a house at the same time, or those who cannot travel, or if you simply miss the bit of fuss at home, why not organise a wedding party? This need not be a sit-down meal or a fancy buffet; an evening party with some finger food and music would do the job. You could tie in your destination as the party theme using music, food and clothes. If it is a return party you can wear your wedding attire and perhaps display your video or album. If it is before the wedding it could be a large engagement celebration.

Cons

Details Some weddings abroad will require more organising than if you stayed at home. Far-flung destinations can bring with them far-flung problems to solve. Negotiating prices through a language barrier can also add to stress.

Guests It is best to make it clear at the outset that no one is expected to travel and that they should feel no pressure to do so. Before finalising your decision you should test the water by chatting to the guests you really want to share the day with. If your sister is buying a house or simply cannot afford to go, will it ruin your day? Everyone you want there may not be able to attend. You may also need to consider paying for guests whom you would like there but who do not have an income, such as an elderly parent or student sibling.

Affordable? Without proper research and good organisation, a wedding abroad may not save you money.

Risk If you cannot afford to travel to your chosen destination in advance, you will need a lot of recommendations and to place your trust in your venue and suppliers. There is an added element of risk.

Long Haul — Las Vegas, Thailand, Caribbean Islands . . .
☺ Legally often more straightforward.
☺ Guaranteed beautiful weather for most of the year.
☺ Cheap high quality goods and services.
☺ Excellent package deals in top class resorts e.g. *sandals.com*.
☹ Injections.
☹ Package deals may not be as unique as you would like.
☹ Not as easy for family and friends to be there, longer flights, higher fares.

Short Haul — Europe: Paris, Amalfi coast, Austrian slopes . . .

☺ Easier for family and friends to be there, shorter flights, cheaper fares.

☺ Amazing choice from snowy hills, white sand beaches to Roman ruins.

☺ No injections (but watch the water).

☹ Possible lengthy legal procedures or awkward residency requirements.

☹ Prices may not be as cheap as you would like.

☹ Weather not as predictable as going to some long-haul destinations.

> To check out exchange rates to see if you are getting a good deal, see *xe.com*.

> Remember that the average present given by a couple is €150. Short-haul, low-fare prices might cover the cost of the flight! So perhaps you could suggest they use this for their flight.

🕐 Good Timing

Preparations Advance planning of at least six months is advisable for a wedding abroad in order to complete paperwork and book services. Plus, the more time you give your guests to save the better.

Off season Like any holiday, everything will be cheaper in the off season, during term time or when the weather is not as good as usual. However, even during the off season there are many destinations where the weather remains very predictable. Remember, many tips for getting married on a budget also apply abroad, such as it being cheaper to marry on a weekday.

Booking

Legal matters You will need to ensure that the wedding you are booking will result in a recognised marriage in Ireland. When choosing a country you should contact the relevant embassy, which should be able to provide you with information on legal requirements and documents, and point you in the right direction for your bookings.

Touch base first with your local travel agent. This will be simply to get brochures, chat about price estimates and for advice on what steps to take.

You should not book the entire wedding through your first point of contact; instead do a lot of research to be sure you are getting the best price on offer.

Tour operators – specialist wedding packages

Many couples choose to contact tour operators offering wedding packages. For long-haul destinations (Caribbean, Maldives), the specialist organiser is invaluable, organising the entire event for you. Everything is taken care of — flights, transfers, accommodation and all the wedding details. Ideal for just a couple or a small group and the prices can be reasonable. Some basic add-ons in packages include a bouquet, cake and champagne. Ceremonies can be carried out on a beach or a bower in hotel gardens. This is the simplest option for a hassle-free wedding, though it may lack in uniqueness.

- Check legal status and insurance.
- How many weddings a day?
- In case of rain can the wedding be postponed for another day or can it go indoors?

Wedding specialists

The more expensive option, wedding specialists offer weddings that are a little more individual, perhaps an unusual venue or tailor-made ceremony. For some countries you might need an expert service if you are planning to marry where it's harder for non-residents to organise (e.g., Italy can be tricky with a lot of red tape, see *italianweddings.ie*).

☺ Self-sufficient

When booking a wedding abroad there is always the option of by-passing the tour operators and booking it all yourself. This requires a large amount of research and planning, from church fees to licence to residency requirements. You will also need to be realistic about the time you are prepared to commit to co-ordinating all aspects of the wedding from home. Thankfully travel more than anything has evolved with the arrival of the internet, and with research you can slice the prices you see in a glossy honeymoon magazine. You can book your entire wedding from the comfort of your living room. Trust the internet here. It can help slash spending if used wisely. Make sure to speak to someone who got married in the venue you are considering.

 **Clever Tips**

Tell everyone you are honeymooners There are discounts and upgrades galore if you use the newlywed card.

Witnesses You will need two witnesses to the wedding. Some hotels charge a small fee for providing witnesses.

Friends left out? Why not organise a really sensational stag or hen (or joint!) in Barcelona, Prague or Paris. That way all your friends get to join in your celebration.

Ring exchanging party Civil ceremonies do not require that you exchange rings, so you could 'get married' abroad and on return throw an 'exchange of rings party'. This could mean everyone back home feels part of your wedding. Dressed in your wedding dress and suit with some beautiful music, your rings are blessed or someone reads a poem while you exchange rings. So romantic!

Examples

Paphos, Greek Island An excellent example of a location abroad is Zucchini's restaurant in Paphos. This company are very highly recommended on the internet by satisfied couples — one woman commented: 'The owner Kim will organise all the details on the Greek end from transport, flowers, hair, makeup, photos, DJ, to Greek dancers and cake. She is English and she and her team are the nicest people ever!' See *zucchiniweddings.com*.

Barbados This is somewhere you can have an idyllic beach wedding. To see an example and some beautiful photographs, check out *coconut-court.com*. Many resorts like Coconut Court have a wedding coordinator who will assist you in planning anything you need. Flights to Barbados for adults range from €700 to €800 depending on when you fly. For children expect to pay approximately €400. Many resorts on the island are very reasonably priced. Another example is *bahamabeachclub.com*.

◖D Something Different

For some, travelling abroad is still not nearly exciting enough. Some crave adventure and a wedding that will be remembered for more than just the cake — for the feeling of standing on a glacier or the wind in your hair as you say your vows in the sky, or even holding a seaweed and coral bouquet under the ocean! There really are too many to choose from across the world but here is a taste of what is on offer if you really do want a *different* wedding.

Hot-air balloon over Las Vegas You are collected in a limo and brought to the launch site for the wedding. Package includes balloon with pilot and crew, and a minister. You must obtain your marriage licence beforehand. See *alittlewhitechapel.com* — $1,000 (€790) per couple.

Fijian raft and waterfall wedding Traditional Fijian ceremony at the gorgeous Maravu Resort on Taveuni Island in Fiji. The bride is brought on a bamboo raft across the deep blue water, which laps over purple corals. Once ashore, she and her partner exchange vows in the rainforest beside a tropical waterfall. The deluxe package includes a Fijian minister, a cake, a bouquet for the bride, neck garlands, decorations, registration and certification fees, choir, dancers, the Maravu Band Boys, wedding feast and champagne for two. See *maravu.net* — cost US$1,250 (€990) for deluxe package but prices start at US$750 (€590).

Glacier wedding In Alaska! Pearson's Pond Luxury Inn and Adventure Spa is named No. 4 World's Most Romantic Destination by *MSN.com*. Package prices range from a wedding at the resort for CA$1,500 (€1,059) rising to $4,500 (€3,117) for a wedding **on top** of an Alaskan glacier! Imagine sharing your vows on top of the spectacular Glacier Ice Fields. The wedding begins in Juneau where you are picked up in your wedding attire, shuttled to the heli-pad and whisked away with photographer and marriage commissioner for the flight to the dramatic Herbert or Mendenhall Glacier. You will fly over glacier icefalls and clear blue crevasses to land on a safe and smooth area for your wedding ceremony. As the helicopter sets down, you will exchange personalised wedding vows during a ceremony. Followed by a champagne reception, cake and first dance on ice. See *pearsonspond.com*.

Fairytale wedding day Why not have a Disney wedding? See *disneyweddings.com*. This site is excellent and you can see how other couples did it. It all looks surprisingly stylish!

Mountaintop wedding in the land of *Lord of the Rings* fame, New Zealand. Love the unique feeling that you are the only people on earth. If this is what you have envisioned for your wedding day, then here is the perfect venue. You will fly via helicopter and land on a peak approx 5,400 above sea level. Here you will have the views of the Southern Alps and the Canterbury Plains. Winter or summer the scenery is breathtaking. See *weddingsnewzealand.com*.

Dolphin delight Exchange your vows in the warm waters of Key Largo in Florida, with two dolphins acting as best man and bridesmaid! You'll even get the ring handed over by a dolphin. The wedding package includes a natural swim session for bride and groom and up to four 'swimming guests' and four observers. Also available for an extra charge are photographs, videos, champagne, flowers and sunset cruises. See *dolphinsplus.com* — cost US$900 (€710).

Webguide

alittlewhitechapel.com
bahamasbeachclub.com
barefootluxury.com
biddingfortravel.com, priceline.com
coconut-court.com
deckchair.com
disneyweddings.com
dolphinsplus.com
guerba.co.uk
italianweddings.ie
lastminute.ie
maravu.net
needahotel.com
pearsonspond.com
sandals.com

trailfinders.ie
weddings.co.uk
weddingsguide.co.uk
weddingsnewzealand.com
xe.com
zucchiniweddings.com

Irish companies
Planning a Rome wedding? First visit *irishcollege.org/wedding*
italianweddings.ie
pragueweddings.ie

UK companies
Cosmos Dream Weddings *cosmos-holidays.co.uk*
First Choice *firstchoice.co.uk*
Hayes and Jarvis *hayers-jarvis.com*
Kuoni *kunoi.co.uk/weddings*
Olympic Holidays *olympicholidays.co.uk*
Virgin Holidays *virginholidays.co.uk/weddings*

Resorts offering free weddings
couples.com
sandals.co.uk
superclubs.org

Other
italiandreamevents.com
italianweddings.ie
marriageitalianstyle.com
mycypruswedding.com
yourdreamweddinginspain.com

Chapter Twenty-Two

The Honeymoon

The focus tends to be held so firmly on the wedding that the honeymoon becomes an enjoyable sideline. Planning your first holiday as a couple is very exciting. Even if your budget is limited, you will still want to feel like you have done something special for your honeymoon. This will involve more than a couple of phone calls and emails but this is the area where you can save most through research and negotiation.

✻ First Decisions

You can plan ahead After spending a lot of money on a wedding there is often little left over for a luxury trip. Why not have a week in the Spanish sun or a few nights in a health spa and instead plan an anniversary trip of a lifetime? You will be left with eleven months to save. It would be a wonderful way to bookend your first year of marriage.

Set up a wedding fund Places like Trailfinders now have wedding list services where guests can pay into your honeymoon account.

Short haul

Ireland Take a camper van around Ireland! With the money you save on flights you can enjoy a journey of discovery eating in the nicest restaurants, staying in country houses or five-star hotels. Check out Georgina Campbell's *Romantic Weddings and Honeymoons*. With a little research it might surprise you just how much there is to see and do right here at home.

UK You can fly or sail very cheaply to the UK. There are fantastic deals, especially off season, to stay in health spas, country retreats, even five-star hotels. As a honeymoon couple from Ireland you are guaranteed to be treated like royalty.

Europe The range of possibilities opened to people with the arrival of cheap airlines deserves a book of its own. For example, a cheap flight to London and a trip on the Eurostar will bring you to the most romantic city in the world!

Long haul

Many of the world's most awe-inspiring sights are located in the world's cheapest countries. Think of all the great man-made monuments: The Taj Mahal, the Great Pyramids, Macchu Pichu, and all the Roman ruins scattered outside Rome. Or if you prefer natural wonders, you can explore the most unspoiled rainforests, go white water rafting, hike up volcanoes, relax on some of the world's most amazing beaches. If you search out a good deal on getting there, using the internet, bargaining, flying at the cheapest time, then it doesn't have to cost the earth to stay there.

Also, the less money you spend the more likely you are to interact with the people who actually live in the place you visit, rather than just other tourists. You'll also get much better deals on everything making individual deals rather than a full package. Plus, packages are often tied to chain hotels which look the same everywhere. With a little bit of effort, and if you visit the right destinations, you'll eat great meals, experience wonderful things, meet people you'll never forget, and come back with photos that'll amaze your friends and family — for a lot less than you think. Of course, the downside is that cheaper holidays are usually cheap because the country and its people are often quite poor relative to our existence. With that there is the need for vaccinations, safety issues on road use and possible crime issues of particular worry to tourists. However, the positives of investing in the local economy, the excitment of living the life and meeting new people in such different parts of the world, are not only immensely enjoyable, but will also leave you appreciating that most of the world's people lead happy lives having just a fraction of what we spend our money on, putting most wedding budget worries into perspective.

☺ Self-sufficient

It is common knowledge that by booking your own holiday you can knock hundreds of euro off package deals. So much so that a recent BBC travel show investigated the theory by opening a travel brochure and booking identical holidays by bargaining directly over the phone or the net, making savings of hundreds of pounds every time. The only disadvantage is you are not covered by package holiday insurance; however, considering the savings it is worth going it alone and arranging your own insurance online. See *bbc.co.uk/holiday*.

🕐 Good Timing

Getting married off peak not only ensures you a cheaper wedding but, even more dramatically, a cheaper honeymoon. Off peak will suit you if you prefer to travel when it is milder weather in hot countries, although you may find some places are very quiet off peak.

◑ Something Different

Life skills If you are not interested in lazing by a pool or taking to the slopes, maybe you would like to go on a learning holiday. You can book cheap flights to Spain and enjoy a week of relaxing on the beach followed by a week of exploring your talents together! How about a yoga, painting or photography holiday? See *andalucian-adventures.co.uk*.

Never skied? Why not learn! Skiing in Serbia offers a cheap alternative for a skiing holiday. See *thomson-ski.co.uk*.

Are you a foodie? Take a cookery course. Visit *tastingplaces.com*.

Learn to sail on the Isle of Wight. See *redfunnelholidays.co.uk*.

Honeymoon romance Write a romantic novel together in a hideaway in Scotland. See *castleofpark.net*. The beautiful and historic Castle of Park, hidden away in a secluded tree-lined park near the Moray coast in northeast Scotland, is known for its warm hospitality, great food and elegant accommodation. Park is famous for its first-rate painting courses/holidays, creative writing courses and photography courses, its castle parties, and, of course, unforgettable castle weddings.

Polish romance The Polish Riviera extends for several hundred kilometres from the German border to Gdansk, along the country's Baltic coastline. It is a favourite summer destination of Poles, but foreign interest is on the increase with holidaymakers seeking low prices and undiscovered beaches. You can fly direct to Gdansk with Ryanair from Dublin. See *visitpoland.org*, *ryanair.com* and *centralwings.com*.

> We went to Fuerteventura in the Canaries for our honeymoon, on a relatively low-budget package. We chose it because it was cheap but quiet and really beautiful. It was also much closer than many of the 'traditional' luxury honeymoon destinations, so a long journey and jet lag weren't a factor after the exhaustion of a wedding. It was great; we slept for a few days, getting over the wedding, and then wandered around, ate lovely food, hired a car and explored. I felt, also, that there was no 'pressure' on the holiday to be absolutely wonderful, if you know what I mean, because we hadn't spent much and hadn't picked somewhere 'idyllic'. So we just enjoyed it, immensely.
>
> **Vanya, Dublin**

 **Clever Tips**

Internet If you have somewhere in mind, rather than clogging up your coffee table with glossy one-sided brochures, why not do an internet search?

The internet has changed travel; good research and preparation knock hundreds, even thousands, off your bill.

Newspaper searches Most broadsheets carry travel supplements at least once a week. These supplements are excellent sources of budget travel tips. Have a look at the English papers too. These have huge resources in comparison to Irish papers and as a result many have extremely well-researched travel sections. Search the sites *travel.guardian.co.uk, travel.timesonline.co.uk, telegraph.co.uk* using the terms 'budget' and 'honeymoon ideas' and you will probably be reading for a week.

Library Remember this valuable resource on your doorstep. Most libraries have excellent travel sections, and if they don't have the book you are looking for they will be more than happy to order it in.

Eco-Ethical Eye

Air travel is one of the biggest pollutants in the world today. People are choosing to holiday locally on principle, knowing how much damage their annual holiday is doing to the environment. Choosing to holiday locally saves on airfares as well as air pollutants.

Take the train The romance of train travel and the romance of Europe's most spectacular scenery combine to create wonderful honeymoons.

- **Le Spezia to Cinque Terre, Italy's North Coast** Referred to as the Bay of Poets, the area surrounding the Italian coastal resort of La Spezia was much loved by romantic poets Shelley, Keats and Byron. It has Italy's most spectacular sections of coastal railway, travelling through tunnels to the Unesco World Heritage site of Cinque Terre.

- **The West Highland Line, the Scottish Highlands** This is one of the world's most memorable train journeys. On a route that takes you far from Glasgow you cross a landscape of moors, mountains, lochs and glens. Tick off some of Scotland's most famous landmarks along the way as the train skirts the River Clyde and Loch Lomond, passes through Crannoch Wood and over Rannoch Moor, passes by Ben Arthur and Ben Nevis and offers views of the islands of Rum and Eigg.

Before the train pulls into its final destination of the harbour town of Mallaig, it has to navigate Glenfinnan viaduct from the *Harry Potter* films. See *scotrail.co.uk*.

⌒⌐ **Webguide**

(See also relevant websites in Chapter Twenty-One.)
andalucian-adventures.co.uk
bbc.co.uk/holiday
biddingfortravel.com, priceline.com
castleofpark.net
centralwings.com
honeypot.ie
lastminute.ie
needahotel.com
redfunnelholidays.co.uk
ryanair.com
scotrail.co.uk
tastingplaces.com
telegraph.co.uk
thomson-ski.co.uk
trailfinders.ie
travel.guardian.co.uk
travel.timesonline.co.uk
travelsupermarket.com
visitnorthernireland.com
visitpoland.org

Chapter Twenty-Three

How to Have a Champagne Hen on a Buck's Fizz Budget

Jenni Woolfson, Director, *poshfizz.com*

Jenni started Posh Fizz as a result of all the difficulties she encountered whilst trying to plan a friend's hen party. The planning and the execution of the weekend was a full-time job and at times she wished that someone else could do it for her. That's when she realised that there was a niche in the market and that many girls would have experienced the same headaches as her. And so, Posh Fizz was launched! The company deals exclusively with ladies-only events and promises to offer the best value that money can buy. Jenni negotiates best prices with all the suppliers and she knows what works and what doesn't! Once the hens can provide approximate information, Jenni gets to work on various weekend proposals. She organises everything from invitations to transport,  accommodation to restaurants, daytime activities to cocktail choices at an extremely affordable price.

Here she shares her tricks dealing with suppliers, finding value for money, and how you can have a Champagne Hen on a Buck's Fizz Budget. Before you start thinking about what your hen party will entail, there are a couple of preliminary steps to take.

1. The organiser

Traditionally, the bridesmaids have the honour of organising the hen party, although these days the bride often chooses another friend or family member to do it. If you don't want to be dressed up in veils, tiaras and L-plates, make sure you choose someone who will respect your wishes! Many brides like to have an input, so let the organiser know how much or how little involvement you want.

2. The guests

Give the organiser all the contact details for those on the guest list as early as possible.

3. The weekend

Decide on two weekends and ask your guests which suits them best. Pick the most popular one, tell everyone to put it in their diary and don't change it unless you absolutely have to!

4. The budget

Hen weekends can cost anything from €100 to €1,000, so you need to be organised! Many people only think of transport and accommodation when they are coming up with their budget. Remember that you also have to eat, drink and play! So make a list of *everything* involved in the weekend — invitations, transport, accommodation, breakfast, lunch, dinner, alcohol, daytime activities and night-time activities. Explain your budget to your friends and check that they are all happy to spend the same amount as you.

Now it's time to get your thinking cap on. To create a fabulous weekend on a budget requires creativity and lots of it! Here are the top tips!

1. Location, location, location

Decide whether or not you want to travel abroad. Many people have the misconception that it is cheaper to go away for their hen weekend. This is not necessarily true, as by staying in your home country you can avoid taking time off work. You can also drive to your venue. If you plan to stay home, don't choose a county that entails a six-hour drive! Stay within two hours from home. After all, you don't want people to be tired from travelling. If you choose to go abroad, remember to look into exchange rates. For example, the UK can be pricey due to the current foreign exchange climate.

2. Accommodation

You will never get a five-star hotel for €40 per person per night in Ireland, but you may get a four-star guest house. Remember, hotels often charge less midweek and off season, so avoid the summer months if you can. And feel free to haggle — what have you got to lose? If you plan to stay there for two nights, ask about a reduced charge to eat in the restaurant or to avail of spa treatments. If you don't ask, you won't get!

Don't rule out the self-catering option. It's often cheaper and is great for noisier hens, as you have no hotel noise restrictions to worry about. Many owners will ask for a deposit, so on arrival put any breakables into cupboards and tidy up after yourselves at the end. This way, you're guaranteed to get the full deposit back.

3. Arrival reception

Crave a champagne reception waiting for your arrival at the hotel? On a tight budget, this is not going to be feasible. So why not ask your hosts to provide a pink lemonade and white wine spritzer reception? It's a tenth of the cost and a lot more interesting than sparkling wine! Don't be afraid to ask your accommodation hosts if they can do anything on your arrival for no charge. You'd be amazed what some will offer.

4. The first night

Think cheap and cheerful for your first night. There may be guests unknown to each other, so you want a relaxed and fun atmosphere to break the ice. Ring ahead to the restaurant and ask them to make up a special set-price menu, so that the bill splitting is easy at the end. Make it that extra bit special by pre-sending personalised decorations for the table. For example, blow up funny photos of each of your guests and laminate them. Ask the restaurant to use them as place-mats! Or ask them to send you menu details and make up your own menu cards for the table.

5. Daytime entertainment

When planning the hen, everyone forgets about the daytime, but this is where you can really add a sparkle to your weekend. Gone are the days where the pub crawl starts when the pubs open! Check out cultural options such as open-top bus tours or brewery visits. If you want something a little more light-hearted, why not ask around in the pubs for a cocktail-making lesson or find a chocolate-tasting afternoon! Enlist the help of a caricaturist to give you drawing lessons or get a tarot card reader to come to you. There are so many fun alternatives.

6. The big night

The second night is often the biggie. Many hens go back to the same restaurant as the previous night. Don't do it! A second time is never the same as the first. It's much better to find an alternative. Many nightclubs have restaurants attached. Contact them in advance to ask about free nightclub entrance if you eat in their restaurant. They can only say no! You should once again try to personalise the meal. Ask the restaurant if they have a secluded area which can be decorated in all things hen! Strippers are so last year, so try to think of something different. How about a 'drunken waiter' or an 'uninvited guest' making a nuisance of themselves?

7. Night-time entertainment

Many brides want something different than going to a night-club for their last night of freedom, so why not look into comedy clubs as an alternative? Many of them have restaurants attached, so no one will get lost in between events! Alternatively, talk to the accommodation owners about transforming a room into a Moulin Rouge style or Bollywood style venue. Have a belly dancing lesson followed by a Turkish meal for example. Go to fabric stores and look at their remnants for inspiration. Remember — use your imagination!

Resources

Chapter Twenty-Four

Research Tools and Web Summary

To really benefit from the tips I offer you in this book, you should add your own local research. Talk to couples who have been married recently, especially those who had weddings that appealed to you. Workmates and friends of your age will most likely be going to several weddings a year too, so chat to them about the venues, the food, the decor. Phone around. Use the internet. Visit message boards and post questions; these online communities are virtual swap shops for ideas.

Research Tools

For the first steps in arranging a church wedding, see *gettingmarried.ie*.

For a civil ceremony see *gronireland.ie.*
For any weddings in the Northern Ireland see *groni.gov.uk.*

Books

Bookshops are bloated with sections on wedding etiquette, guides to speeches, religious preparation and flower arranging. All very nice but hardly a priority for most couples. Here are some refreshing and to-the-point information sources for budding wedding planners.

Georgina Campbell's Ireland for Romantic Weddings and Honeymoons (2006)/ireland-guide.com

Recently published, this photo-filled book is an excellent aid in choosing your venue. As well as breaking down the basic preparations needed to get your plans moving, it looks at restaurants, hotels, country houses, castles and rural retreats to consider as your reception venue or honeymoon getaway. All venues are included on merit alone, entry is free and establishments may not pay for inclusion, or advertise, in the guide. For someone working to a budget it answers all the essential questions: Can I bring my own wine? Can I serve cake as dessert? Working county by county, including Northern Ireland, each venue is described and summarised, detailing prices, venue capacity, flowers, corkage, accommodation, service charges, amenities and activities. For those of you starting your search for the perfect venue I would certainly recommend this book.

DOT.ie: A Practical Guide to Using the Internet in Ireland by Alex French

If you are not online and the thought frightens you, or even if you are online but the thought of purchasing something online or posting on a message board frightens you, I recommend this book. Covering topics such as getting online, the basics of web browsing and email, online travel and shopping, chatting online, viruses and phishing, this will come in very handy during the organising of your wedding and will continue to be useful long after the day is over.

Irish Bride's Survival Guide by Natasha Mac a Bháird

This book is helpful in that it brings you through the legal and religious requirements specific to Irish weddings. It also takes you through your ceremony step by step and helps with problem-solving for your day.

A Wedding of Your Own by Padraig McCarthy

This book has received good reviews. McCarthy says that in the rush of practical preparations, it is easy to neglect emotional preparation for a Catholic wedding and marriage. *A Wedding of Your Own* explains the entire wedding ceremony in detail, allowing each couple to make their wedding unique and personally meaningful.

Local libraries are great resources for all the books listed and further books on flower arranging, table decoration, getting married abroad, wedding speeches, travel guides (see *library.ie*).

Budgeting

The TAB Guide by Sandra Gannon, Jill Kerby and Neil Brooks (*tab.ie*)

This guide explains to you in plain English how you can make the most of your money and the least of your tax payments. It explains investment opportunities and a wide range of other financial matters.

askaboutmoney.com This is a discussion forum/community about all things financial. It is overseen by a team of volunteer moderators. The moderators are regular contributors and they also develop and promote the site. They don't accept advertising, sponsorships or kickbacks of any sort. Users contribute to running costs. There are regular discussions about financing your wedding.

Wedding Sites

In wedding-related websites, you won't find critical reviews of services or venues in the main part of the website because the website is like a shop, it is in the business of selling, not losing advertisers or potential advertisers. However, you will find some great articles, tips on questions to ask your venue, speeches, and brides' diaries. The '*ask the experts*' sections can be very helpful but it is good to remember the main motivation is to encourage you to spend, spend, spend . . . and the experts are often also advertisers!

Irish sites

smartbride.ie This customer-focused website was launched in conjunction with this book. Log on for more tips, articles, real life stories, web links and of course, chat!

weddingsonline.ie Very busy site. Recently revamped. Large supplier directory. Major web community of brides. Good to-the-point articles and handy downloads. However, the advertising spills into the discussion forum, with T-shirts advertised 'within' posts, which is very irritating.

simplyweddings.com Stylish looking site, and very easy to navigate. The discussion forums are quieter than those on *weddingsonline.ie* but feel a little friendlier! Great planning section. Some of the articles are good but many seem quite random, slightly anti-men in parts and can be quite clichéd.

There are other Irish weddings sites but they are generally very dated in style, hard to navigate and contain more advertising listings than anything useful.

ivoryandlace.com Ivory and Lace is a new wedding directory beautifully designed to make the search for wedding-related services as straightforward as possible.

UK sites

Two major websites in the UK are Hitched (*hitched.co.uk*) and Confetti (*confetti.co.uk*), excellent sites for all aspects of your planning.

US sites

The main wedding website in the US is The Knot (*theknot.com*), worth a look for the brides' stories alone. Weddings are big business in the US.

Message boards

The message boards on these websites have a **search facility** which allows you to weed out the information you need from this hive of chit-chat, recommendations, debate and quite a few fiery arguments! You can register, choosing an online alias such as 'LaoisBride' and ask your own questions with anonymity. It is best to do a topic search before posting a message as your question has probably been answered many times before.

Message board savvy:

- Always remember that other people's opinions on what is tasteful or good quality may not be similar to yours, so be sure to look for more than one recommendation.
- If you are very sensitive I would not recommend posting photographs or very private information on message boards. Manners are regularly forgotten when people are posting from behind a keyboard. I've seen many brides' happy wedding day photos or plans for their day rudely insulted on these message boards.
- Remember too that without the nuance of the spoken word it is easy to be taken up wrong. It is best to be careful how you put across your opinion, and it is recommended that you use those funny smiley faces ('emoticons') to let the other poster know if you are being sarcastic, joking, etc.
- Also, you will soon become accustomed to the abbreviations used, such as DH (darling husband), DS/DD (darling son/daughter), BM (bridesmaid), SIL (sister-in-law, etc.), BTW (by the way), IMO (in my opinion), IMHO (in my humble opinion), IYKWIM (if you know what I mean), TMI (too much information), LOL (lots of laughter), ROFL (rolling on the floor laughing).

But, these boards are also full of tonnes of friendly people and fun conversations, and brides regularly meet up, sometimes becoming friends for life!

Web Summary

Chapter One: The Anatomy of a Wedding

daft.ie
nixers.com

revenue.ie

Chapter Two: Shopping: General Tips

amazon.com
askaboutmoney.com
bbbonline.org
debenhamsweddings.com
ebay.ie
eccdublin.ie
goldenpages.ie
gettingmarried.ie
groireland.ie
groni.gov.uk
hitched.co.uk

ivoryandlace.com
marksandspencer.com
monsoon.co.uk
myus.com
nextdirectory.ie
safecard.ie
simplyweddings.com
tab.ie
theknot.com
weddingsonline.ie
xe.com

Chapter Three: The Ceremony

benedictinemonks.co.uk
citizensinformation.ie
confettidirect.co.uk
gettingmarried.ie
groireland.ie
groni.gov.uk

irish-humanists.org
myweddingbox.co.uk
reasonableribbon.com
xena-productions.com
webwedding.co.uk

Chapter Four: The Reception Venue

ballyhannon-castle.com
cccdub.ie
goireland.com
hiddenireland.com
inishboffin.com
ireland-guide.com
irelandsbluebook.com

irishgems.com
irishluxury.com
marquee.ie
rectoryglandore.com
venuesearch.ie
weddingsathome.ie

Chapter Five: Food

bbc.co.uk/food
odlums.ie

tasteofireland.com

Chapter Six: Champagne, Buck's Fizz and Wine

fairtrade.org.uk
mywine.ie
tasteofireland.com

thewineroom.ie
traidcraft.co.uk
wineandbeerworld.com

Chapter Seven: The Cake

cakebox.ie
cakesonline.ie
claycorner.co.uk
crumbsanddoilies.co.uk

eveningclasses.ie
polymerclaypit.co.uk
sheridanscheesemongers.com
the-cake-gallery.com

Chapter Eight: Entertainment

irishweddingdj.com

iTunes.com

Chapter Nine: The Dress

barnardos.ie
bridalsales.ie
bridesave.com
buyandsell.ie
carnmeal.com
dreambridal.ie
gownsales.com
groups.yahoo.com/group/leinsterfreecycle

hillcrestbridal.co.uk
houseofbrides.com
jumbletown.ie
netbride.com
organicsilks.co.uk
oxfamireland.org
weddingsonline.ie/discussion
xe.com

Chapter Ten: The Bridal Party

lantz.ie/accessories

rkbridal.com

Chapter Eleven: Accessories

eveningcourses.ie
faux.uk.com
glamgal.com

ncad.ie
theweddingshop.ie

Chapter Twelve: Ten Things About Rings

diamond.ie
diamondsandgoldireland.com
e-weddingbands.com

nodirtygold.org
silverchilli.com
touchwoodrings.com

Chapter Thirteen: Shoes

bridalshoes.co.uk

face2.ie

Chapter Fourteen: Flowers and Decorations

caradandesigns.com
carnmeal.com
englishplants.co.uk
eveningcourses.ie

flowers.org.uk
hibiscusflorals.com
theknot.com
wedideas.com

Chapter Fifteen: Favours

amnesty.ie
cakesandfavours.com
cancer.ie
carnmeal.com
chezemily.ie
diywedding.ie

lantz.ie
rspca.org.uk
stick-n-mix.co.uk
traidcraft.co.uk
weddingcrafter.co.uk

Chapter Sixteen: Themes and Inspirations

brideandgroomdirect.co.uk

chezemily.ie

chocolate.co.uk

cocochocolate.co.uk

coxandcox.co.uk

http://bios.magnificentbliss.com

marthastewart.com

organicweddings.com

the-chocolate-fountain-company.com

theknot.com

theweddingshop.ie

weddingsbyfranc.com

xena-productions.com

Chapter Seventeen: Stationery

bonusprint.co.uk

brideandgroomdirect.co.uk

clifforddesigns.ie

craftfactory.ie

craftsupplies.ie

daintree.ie

debenhamsweddings.com

diywedding.ie

eco-wedding.com

google.ie/picasa

haveandhold.co.uk

kodakgallery.eu

marksandspencer.com

messageinabottle.com

photobox.ie

pixdiscount.com

rps.gn.apc.org

shutterfly.com

Chapter Eighteen: The Car

carboncalculator.com

goldenpages.ie

iwantoneofthose.com

Chapter Nineteen: Photography

aspinaloflondon.com

irishphotographers.com

katespaperie.com

newbridgesilverware.com

Chapter Twenty: Video/DVD

download.com

pixmania.com

which.co.uk

Chapter Twenty-One: Getting Married Abroad

alittlewhitechapel.com

bahamasbeachclub.com

barefootluxury.com

biddingfortravel.com

coconut-court.com

cosmos-holidays.co.uk

couples.com

deckchair.com

disneyweddings.com

dolphinsplus.com

firstchoice.co.uk

guerba.co.uk

hayes-jarvis.co.uk

irishcollege.org/wedding (Italy)

italiandreamevents.com

italianweddings.ie

kuoni.co.uk/weddings

lastminute.com

maravu.net

marriageitalianstyle.com

mycypruswedding.com

needahotel.com

olympic.holidays.co.uk

pearsonpond.com

pragueweddings.ie

priceline.com

sandals.com

superclubs.org

trailfinders.ie

virginholidays.co.uk/weddings

weddingguide.ie

weddings.co.uk

weddingsnewzealand.com

xe.com

yourdreamweddinginspain.com

zucchiniweddings.com

Chapter Twenty-Two: The Honeymoon

andalucian-adventures.co.uk

bbc.co.uk/holiday

biddingfortravel.com

castleofpark.net

centralwings.com

edfunnelholidays.co.uk

honeypot.ie

lastminute.ie

needahotel.com

priceline.com

ryanair.com

rvisitpoland.org

scotrail.co.uk

tastingplaces.com

telegraph.co.uk

thomson-ski.co.uk

trailfinders.ie

travel.guardian.co.uk

travel.timesonline.co.uk

travelsupermarket.com

visitnorthernireland.com

Index

abroad, marrying abroad, 9, 17,
    155–63
    cost, 155–6
    parties, 125, 156–7, 160
    shoes, 93
    websites, 186
accessories, 14, 84–6
    websites, 183–4
Accessorize, 14, 85
accommodation, 31–2, 39
Alaska, 161
Apassionata Flowers, 115–19
Arnott's, 14

balloons, 112
balloons, hot-air, 161
Ballyhannon Castle, 37
bank holidays, 8
Barbados, 160
Barnados, 77
beads, as hair decorations, 86
Beck, Janet, 149–51
Benedictine monks, candle-making,
    25–6
biography pages, 127
blessings, 20–21
booklets, 130–31, 132
books, 12, 178–9
borrowing money, 6, 14
bouquets, 107–8, 115, 118
    bridesmaids, 115
    crystal bouquets, 113
    diamante into the bouquet, 112
    simplicity, 105
    thank-you-mum, 118
    see also flowers
bridalwear, 10–14
    websites, 183–4
    see also accessories; dress; shoes

bridesmaids, 81–2
    bouquets, 115
    dresses, 12–13, 81–2
    make-up, 95
    shoes, 93
Brown Thomas, 14
Buck's Fizz, 53
budget see cost and budget
buffets, 44–5
bulbs, flowering, 111
buttonholes, 115

cake, 11–12, 59–64
    cost, 12, 60
    decorations, 61
    self-bake, 60
    served as dessert, 46, 63
    websites, 183
Cakebox, 61
Caldecourt, Andrea, 106, 109
camcorders, 145–51
cameras, disposable, 143, 144
Campbell, Georgina, 30, 38–40, 46,
    63, 165, 178
Canary Islands, 167
candles, 23, 25–6
carpet, red carpet, 24
cars, 135–8
    websites, 185
cash gifts, 5–6, 33
Castle of Park, 167
castles, 31–2, 37, 40
ceremony, 7, 19–28
    decorations, 21, 23–4, 106, 117
    music, 21, 22, 24–5, 27
    websites, 182
champagne, 52, 53, 57–8
charity donations, 122–3
charity shops, 77

cheese wedding cake, 62–3
cheesecake, 62
children
  clothes, 13–14
  flower girls, 13–14, 81–2, 115
  noise, 26
  page boys, 82, 83
chocolate fountain, 126
chocolate theme, 126
chocolates, 122
Christchurch Cathedral, 32
Christmas, 22, 46–7, 64, 111, 121, 125
church ceremonies, 20, 27
  music, 21, 22, 24–5, 27
Cinderella's Bridal Shop, 77
civil ceremonies, 20, 21, 25
Civil Registration Act 2004, 25
Claire's Accessories, 14, 85
Clifford Designs, 132
clubs, 36, 37
cocktail parties, 47
Coconut Court, 160
confetti, 26
Coolbawn Quay, 36, 40
corkage prices, 53
cost and budget, 2–8
  accessories, 85–6
  bargaining with suppliers, 6, 32–3,
    79, 143
  bridesmaids' dresses, 12–13, 81–2
  cars, 136
  entertainment, 65, 68, 70
  flowers, 104, 116
  food, 44–5, 46
  hair, 99
  hen weekends, 171–2
  photography, 141, 151
  shoes, 92, 93
  shopping tips, 10–18
  size of wedding, 5–6, 7–8
  stationery, 129, 131
  videos, 146
  wedding cake, 11–12, 60
  wedding dress, 11, 13, 74, 76–7
  wine, 53–4

Costello and Costello, 85
Costume (boutique), 75
country houses, 32
Cox and Cox, 125
credit cards, 14, 15–16
croque en bouche, 62
crypts, 32
crystal bouquets, 113
cupcake mountain, 61

dancing, 67
date and seasonality, 8
  cake, 64
  ceremony, 22
  favours, 121
  flowers, 105, 109, 111, 118–19
  food, 46–7, 49
  honeymoon, 166
  marrying abroad, 158
  reception venue, 34–5
day of the week, choice of, 8, 34–5, 39
Debenhams, 11, 133
'dessert wedding', 48
diamante into the bouquet, 112
diamonds, 89–90
Disney wedding, 162
DJs, 65–6, 69–70
Dolan, Ben, 149–51
dolphins, Florida wedding, 162
Doonmore Hotel, 31
dress, wedding dress, 73–80
  alterations, 77–8
  buying tips, 11, 13, 74–9
  cost, 11, 13, 74, 76–7
  edible dress, 61
  non-bridal look, 75
  renting, 77
  second-hand, 76–7
  selling on afterwards, 77, 79–80
  sharing, 79
  websites, 183
dressmakers, 78
drinks, 44, 45, 52
  cocktails, 47
  see also wine

drinks reception, 44, 51–2
Dunnes Stores, 57
DVDs, 145–51
    websites, 185

Eason's, 14
Easter, 47, 64, 125
eBay, 16–17, 76
ecological issues
    air travel, 168
    ceremony, 25–6
    flowers, 114
    food, 48
    organic weddings, 127
    stationery, 134
    wine, 55, 57
Encore Bridal, 77
entertainment, 65–70
    cost, 65, 68, 70
    websites, 183
event management companies, 107

Face2 Make-Up, 94, 96
Fairytale Brides (rental shop), 77
fairytale weddings, 126, 162
    castles, 31–2, 37, 40
    horse and carriage, 137
favours, 120–23
    websites, 184
Fay, Tara, 127
feather pens, 14
feathers, 26, 112
. Fiji, 161
finances see cost and budget
Finnegan, Ruairi, 69–70
Florida, 162
flower girls, 13–14, 81–2, 115
flowers, 103–19
    artificial, 113
    ceremony decorations, 21, 23–4,
        106, 117
    choosing a florist, 104–6, 116–17
    cost, 104, 116
    DIY, 107–9, 119
    potted plants, 26

at reception, 106–7, 109, 117–18
    seasonal, 105, 109, 111, 118–19
    sharing, 23
    simplicity, 105
    tips for cut flower care, 109–11
    websites, 184
food, 39, 43–50
    cost, 44–5, 46
    DIY, 45
    organic, 48
    seasonal, 46–7, 49
    websites, 183
foreign exchange, 158
forums, online wedding forums, 10,
    179
French, Alex, 15–18, 178
French fancies, 62
fur, fake fur, 86

Gannon, Sandra, Kerby, Jill and
    Brooks, Neil, 179
gazebos, 35
gifts, cash gifts, 5–6, 33
gifts for guests (favours), 120–23
    websites, 184
glacier wedding, 161
Glandore Rectory, 32
Glass Eye Productions, 149
glasses, 113
Greece, 160
Gribbon, Annie, 94–7
groom
    buttonholes, 115
    clothing, 83
guest books, 12

hair accessories, 85–6
hairdressing, 97–9
hats, 85
helicopters, 137
hen parties, 170–74
    abroad, 160
Hickey's Fabric Stores, 86
High Society, 77
Hobbs, Eddie, 5–6, 33

honeymoons, 164–9
  in Ireland, 40, 165
  websites, 186
horse and carriage, 137
hotels, 31–2
  honeymoons, 165
humanist ceremonies, 21

Inisbofin Island, 31
Internet, 15–18, 177–8
  credit card fraud, 15–16
  message boards, 181
  online forums, 10, 179
  practical guide, 15–18
  web summary, 182–6
investments, 5
invitations, 12, 130, 131–4
iPods, 66
Ireland, honeymoons in, 40, 165
Ireland for Romantic Weddings and Honeymoons, 30, 38, 46, 63, 165, 178
Irish Bride's Survival Guide, 178
Italy, 168
Ivory and Lace, 180
ivy, 111

jewellery, 12, 85 *see also* rings

Kelly, Peter, 127

Las Vegas, 161
late, being late, 22
legal requirements, 20, 25
  marrying abroad, 158
libraries, 179
lingerie, 11
Lismore Castle, 40
loans, 6

Mac a Baird, Natasha, 178
McCarthy, Padraig, 179
magicians, 68
make-up, 94–7
Marks & Spencer, 11–12, 26, 54, 60, 85, 92, 133

marquees, 35–6
men
  buttonholes, 115
  clothes, 83
  hair, 99
message boards, Internet, 181
midweek offers, 34–5
Millen, Karen, 75
mobile phones, 27
money *see* cost and budget
Monsoon, 13–14
mountaintop wedding, 162
Murray, Anthony, 97–9
music
  at ceremony, 21, 22, 24–5, 27
  at reception, 65–70

negotiating with suppliers, 6, 32–3, 79, 143
New Zealand, 162
Next, 12–13
noise, 26–7, 40, 67

O'Briens off-licence, 54, 57
Oddbins, 54
off-licences, 54, 57
organic food, 48
organic weddings, 127
organic wine, 57
outdoor parties, 35–6
Oxfam Occasions, 77

page boys, 82, 83
Paphos, 160
PayPal, 17
pens, 14
petals, 113
  baskets of, 24
photograph albums, 13, 142
photography, 141–4
  copyright, 6
  cost, 141, 151
  photos on stationery, 133
  studio, 142
  websites, 185

place names, 122, 125, 131
plants, potted, 26
Poland, 167
Posh Fizz, 170–71
Practical Guide to Using the Internet in Ireland, 15, 178
practice and rehearsals, 25
priorities, 3–4
profiteroles, 62
punctuality, 22

raft wedding, 161
reception venue, 29–40
  choosing, 8, 29–35, 38–40
  flowers, 106–7, 109, 117–18
  question list, 33–4
  websites, 182
red carpet, 24
registry office, 20, 21, 25
rehearsals, 25
restaurants, 32
ribbon, 23, 112
rings, 87–90
  exchange of, 25
  exchange of rings party, 160
  websites, 184
RSVP cards, 130
Russian dolls, 122

sailing, 167
saving up, 4, 5
Scotland, 167, 168–9
seasonality *see* date and seasonality
Serbia, 167
Sheridans Cheesmongers, 62–3
shoes, 91–3
  websites, 184
shopping, general tips, 10–18
silk flowers, 113
size of wedding, 5–6, 7–8, 39
skiing, 167
Spain, 166
speeches, 46
stamps, 132
stationery, 129–34

cost, 129, 131
DIY, 130, 131–2, 134
websites, 185
Stewart, Martha, 127
stress, 95
  marrying abroad, 156
Superquinn, 54

TAB Guide, 179
table decorations, 47, 113, 118, 121, 125
tans, fake tans, 96
tea, at reception, 44, 45, 52
Tesco, 53, 54, 58
thank you cards, 131
thank you mum bouquets, 118
themes, 124–8
  websites, 185
timing *see* date and seasonality
toasts, 52
toilet cubicles, fun decorations, 68
tour operators, 159
Trailfinders, 165
train journeys, 168
trumpet players, 24
Tullio, Paolo, 56–8

UK Flowers & Plants Association, 106, 109–10

veils, 85–6
venue *see* reception venue
videos, 145–51

waterfall wedding, 161
websites, 179–81
  biography pages, 127
  guide to Internet use, 15–18
  Irish sites, 180
  message boards, 181
  online forums, 10, 179
  web summary, 182–6
Wedding Flowers (magazine), 112
Weddings At Home, 35
Wilson, John, 57

wine, 51–8
  amount to serve, 52
  bring-your-own, 53–4, 55, 56–8
  champagne v wine debate, 52, 53,
    57–8
  choosing, 53–4, 55, 56–8
  cost, 53–4
  drinks reception, 44, 51–2
  frosted glasses, 113
  licence for selling, 36
  spritzer, 172
  websites, 183
wish list, 3–4
Woolfson, Jenni, 170–74

Wishing you a wonderful wedding day and
a long and happy life together!
Sarah
X